THE
SPITFIRE
50 Years On

The long nose and the Griffon growl had very noticeably changed the Spitfire by 1944 when the first Mk XIVs came into use. The distinctive wing planform remained (RAF Museum 5986–5).

THE
SPITFIRE
50 Years On

MICHAEL J.F. BOWYER

 Patrick Stephens, Wellingborough

First published in 1986

British Library Cataloguing in Publication Data

Bowyer, Michael J. F.
    The Spitfire : 50 years on.
    1. Spitfire (Fighter planes)
    I. Title
    623.74'64   UG1242.F5

    ISBN 0–85059–811–7

Patrick Stephens Limited is part of the
Thorsons Publishing Group

Photoset in 9pt and 10 on 11pt Plantin by Avocet Marketing
Services Limited, Bicester, Oxon. Printed in Great Britain by
Anchor Brendon Limited, Tiptree, Colchester, Essex, for the
publishers Patrick Stephens Limited, Denington Estate,
Wellingborough, Northants, NN8 2QD, England.

Contents

Acknowledgments
The author extends his thanks to many people who have
assisted in the production of *The Spitfire: Fifty Years On,*
in particular the RAF Museum, Rolls-Royce, Ernest
Brooks Esq, Robert Brooks Esq, M.H.Evans Esq, John
Strangward Esq, and Alan Wright Esq.

Chapter 1
The Spitfire's spell

'Now, running in from your left, ladies and gentlemen, the Battle of Britain Memorial Flight.' Few aviation displays take place without the appearance of the Lancaster bomber, Hurricane and Spitfire, each aircraft occupying a hallowed place in our heritage. Without those two fighters in particular, the outcome of the Second World War would, without the slightest doubt, have been disastrous for the civilized world.

'Break', and the pair slip away from the big, black bomber and in so doing reveal their utterly different forms. It is immediately apparent that, even after fifty years, one remains steeped in inestimable affection: 'Spitfire' — the name, the image, the sound are as alluring as when half a century, yes an astonishing half century ago, that roar, that utterly unmistakable whistle, became a cry for a seemingly impossible victory.

Meanwhile, the Hurricane has slipped behind a cloud. Rugged, far easier to build, almost as fast, easy to handle, just as strongly armed and the main instrument with which the Royal Air Force won the Battle of Britain, on many counts this rather masculine machine should receive more praise than its sleeker, more curvaceous, more feminine, companion. Our affections are so often not awarded on a logical basis, and frequently are not engendered after ponderous consideration: for most of us a shapely form is instantly irresistible. From the Arctic to the Tropics, over much of the globe, the Hurricane fought a highly distinguished war, performing superbly in the desert and the jungle. A resolute fighter, it contributed brilliantly to many a tough campaign. And yet, during the conflict and certainly since, among those who flew or endured the war and millions too young even to have glimpsed a Spitfire at work, that wondrous form has become legendary. To see, to touch, to remember and surely to have flown a Spitfire is to associate with an idol which, in the worst moments of our entire history, encouraged hope from despair, pride out of disaster.

Just what made this so? Racing towards battle an approaching Spitfire never ceased to bring exhilaration, was ever symbolic of that final victory. Hurrying by, exuding that distinctive whistle culled from a combination of its magic Merlin and fine form, it was something never surpassed. As its eight guns chattered, the combination of throaty engine roar and resounding battle thrilled the soul. And always it was possible to detect, by sound, distant Spitfires pestering the Hun.

All was linked distinctively to a form as beautiful as any that has ever taken to the skies. Sleek, slender body superbly contoured, almost completely curved and thus far from easy to build, led to a nose into which the mighty Merlin neatly disappeared, such wonders to perform. No bulky radiator to cool his ardour, merely a slip of a thing hiding (unusually) beneath a wing. And what a wing! Wafer thin for its time, scarcely thick enough even to contain the guns, its elliptical form, curved leading edge and delicately formed tips made it totally distinctive. Surely nobody, just nobody, could mistake a Spitfire? The wonder remains that so much speed, agility, fire power and sheer excellence could be packed into such a small aeroplane.

As for the sight of a pack of hunting Spitfires, whistling over at roof-top height, straining at full power on the battle climb in that fateful 1940 summer, or neatly packed ready to scour French skies, or guarding a swarm of American bombers, few sights in wartime could equal these. A brace of dawn-flying Spitfires scampering low to detect enemy shipping, a high flyer after a contrailing bomber or a Spitfire aerobatting for sheer joy on a clear blue summer eve, all are scenes indelible. Never to be forgotten is the crackling of the later Merlins, and the chuckling after the chase, and the victory roll before the jubilant Spitfire slipped neatly onto its bumpy, grass home.

Come mid-war and the entire note changed as the prime defender took to the offensive. Shorter wings, longer nose, strange tail, humped canopy, all combined to produce something very different: an aircraft soon consorting with the rumbling Griffon — whose power could only be utilized after cosmetic assistance. Fading, that simple, exquisite sight trading itself for greater power, an astonishing burst of speed, the addition of spy cameras, heavier guns and even bombs. That basic form was quite able to cope with a doubling of its weight and even then improve its performance by as much as a third. For that alone the Spitfire and those who created it deserve the enormous admiration showered upon them.

But whatever was done, wherever it went, the Spitfire would always be remembered (albeit somewhat unfairly) as the fighter that won the Battle of Britain. As the years roll by its legendary spell extends, for this was the fighter of the aces — or so it is generally believed. For such popular beliefs, wartime propaganda and the film *The First of the Few* were largely responsible and that will never change. As Winston Churchill rallied the nation with his war-winning cries on bright summer evenings in 1940 one could not but associate his clarion calls with the image of the Spitfire (sadly, never the Hurricane). Certainly part of the magic was that great man's doing. From the imagery of a mystical bird spitting fire, to the flying product, a result of the merging of great skill and dedication, the spell of the Spitfire was woven.

Chapter 2
A 'super marine' company

Building aeroplanes is always a risky venture. The stakes are high, the cost can be enormous, and the market wavers so much that even the most flourishing manufacturer can suddenly plunge into disaster. Excessive drive, flair and dedicated engineering are needed to create the best product in which attention to detail is of paramount importance for both personal and company survival. Only the well-founded survive for any length of time, doing so as a result of courage, foresight, initiative, skill, intuition and imagination. All these qualities were found within a small aircraft company established shortly before the 1914-18 War.

Anchored near Southampton in the River Itchen lay a three-masted schooner. Aboard lived the imaginative, unconventional Noel Pemberton Billing. Dreams are but for dreamers whereas bright ideas pay the bills. Pemberton Billing experienced both with his desire to combine sailing and flying in a practical, marketable 'flying-boat'. To turn this into reality he acquired an aged coal wharf at close-by Woolston and here, in 1913, he and a handful of others set about building a winged boat. This they called a 'super-marine' craft and soon the name was adopted by their company whose first product, the Supermarine P.B.1 biplane, was placed on exhibition in London during March 1914.

Success rarely arises easily, and Pemberton Billing's boat never flew. Instead, his interest immediately switched to fighting aircraft as the First World War engulfed all before it. His company devised a variety of schemes, before the P.B.9 emerged as a pointer to distant fame. Gathering his small group on the first Monday of the war, Pemberton Billing informed them that this scout aircraft for the Royal Flying Corps was now the firm's main pre-occupation. Such were aeroplanes of those days that by the following Monday, it was complete and able to make its first flight on 12 August 1914.

Pemberton Billing was a restless fellow and, with Hubert Scott-Paine minding the works, he left to serve in the Royal Navy. At Supermarine ideas for further fighters flowed before interest switched in 1915 to a big, unconventional four-wing Zeppelin interceptor, the NightHawk. The company's contribution to the war effort remained limited, but its interest in fighters and seaplanes was to prove of enormous value.

Impetuous Pemberton Billing made no effort to hide his personal feelings upon the conduct of the war, and especially the way in which the RFC was flung into battle flying easily out-fought aeroplanes. Having no say in such proceedings, he decided that he must get himself elected into Parliament. When that was achieved in 1916, Hubert Scott-Paine became managing director of what was now the Supermarine Aviation Works Ltd. Pemberton Billing, a shrewd fellow, had established strong links with the Admiralty, presumably reckoning on a market for his 'flying boats'. Instead, the Navy engaged Supermarine to construct, at the Woolston works, designs produced by their Air Department. The 1916 changes resulted in the company — in which the government now had a hand — being entirely re-structured. Limited expansion included additional buildings but, far, far more important, were new faces. Among them was a twenty-year-old Reginald Joseph Mitchell.

Supermarine now undertook small-scale sub-contracting work, building Norman Thompson and Short flying-boats while the design staff, including Mitchell, tackled the jointly devised Navy and Supermarine Navyplane. Next came the Admiralty's desire for a fighter flying-boat which led Supermarine to design their Baby, a pusher biplane, in which Mitchell was more involved. From this design was to stem a line of flying-boats and amphibians, among them the famous Seagull and Walrus biplanes and not until the late 1940s did Supermarine interest in seaplanes fade. Taxing to design and governed by special requirements, almost all seaplanes had their performances penalized by heavy drag. It was the attempt to reduce this that led to Mitchell's most memorable creations.

Chapter 3
To win the Schneider Trophy

The end of the 1914–18 war brought incredibly fast reductions in Britain's military strength. Aviation, which had made such enormous advances, had its wings clipped abruptly and private flying was very limited. Supermarine decided to invest its future in the development of its wartime flying-boat designs and in 1919 placed its single-engined Sea Lion pusher flying-boat in the Schneider Trophy Race. Devised by Jacques Schneider, the race involved the completion of 150 nautical miles over a six-mile circuit with two landings during the first circuit. There had been two such races pre-war. Supermarine's entry in the 1919 Bournemouth race ended in disaster when the company's entrant hit an obstruction while taking off. By the rules, whoever won the race three times would win the Trophy outright and in 1920 and 1921 Italy was the victor. With government support, more Italian success seemed likely.

Supermarine effort was now concentrated upon refining their initial entrant and in 1922 the Sea Lion II was built at the company's expense to Mitchell's design. The aircraft beat the Italian entry at an average speed of 145.7 mph. Encouraging indeed, but expensive air races could hardly keep the company buoyant. The 1923 race in which the Sea Lion III took part was won by the USA: Supermarine decided that for commercial reasons they needed to commence the design of moderate sized flying-boats but intended to maintain their interest in racing machines which were very useful for research purposes.

Mitchell was already very well aware that the key to faster flying must be improved aerodynamics. The drag could be cut by reducing the aircraft's wetted area, and by decreasing its frontal section. Thin wings, small cross section for the fuselage and the elimination of as many bracing wires and struts as possible were areas of possible improvement to which Mitchell directed his attention.

Achieving all that required a radical plunge into a completely new field for Supermarine — the monoplane floatplane streamlined in the extreme and powered by a close-cowled liquid-cooled engine. The power-to-weight ratio of the latter was of immediate importance, and to achieve the best factor Supermarine and Napier established a partnership from which evolved a version of the well-tried Napier Lion able to give 700 hp for brief periods. After finally casting aside residual ideas for a sleek biplane, Supermarine Schneider No 4 emerged in 1925 as a highly streamlined almost all-wooden floatplane.

Penalties for high-speed flight were at once apparent. Uncomfortably sitting on his bottom, legs outstretched to help reduce the fuselage depth, the pilot experienced extreme discomfort, and his forward view was extremely poor. Thin wings had reduced lift so that getting the aircraft's floats out of the water to sit on their small but vitally important step meant a long run to gather speed, hopefully without hitting even the smallest floating object. It must have been apparent to Mitchell and the Supermarine team that attention to detail was as important for success as quite drastic change, a lesson that was vindicated in the development of the Spitfire. That very rapid introduction of change could bring disaster was also soon shown.

Before leaving for the 1925 Race in the USA, Henri Baird, flying the unbraced wing, cantilever-strutted S.4 at Calshot reached 226.75 mph to capture the world speed record for seaplanes. Then, on the eve of the Trophy Race, disaster struck — a violent tremor overtook the aircraft and high-speed flutter caused it to crash into Chesapeake Bay. It was probably the absence of wire bracing that was responsible; future racers would be thus fitted and attention to such details would feature in design and testing stages. With all fighter aircraft there exists a fear that combat manoeuvres will make destructive demands upon the airframe. It is significant that in the case of the Spitfire there was never any major worry on that score. Lessons learned from the seaplanes were clearly well applied.

While plans to improve the racer evolved, Mitchell was also working upon the design of a new line of flying-boats, led by the Southampton. In later days and in RAF hands this aircraft was to make some spectacular long-distance flights linking Empire outposts, pointing the way for commercial activity, and providing useful experience for military airborne mariners. Useful as all that proved to be, far greater fall-out stemmed from the Schneider racers.

By 1927 the race had become most prestigious with everything to be won. The British government sensing success and the good publicity that would result was keen to be associated with the event, while Supermarine was ever more certain that the key to success lay in reduced drag and weight — and a compact, powerful engine. But the pressures on the structure still demanded a braced or strutted wing. Mitchell chose bracing, an even more reduced fuselage cross section, a tightly-packed pilot and a very neatly installed Napier Lion VIIA/B engine.

An all too apparent problem was produced by the torque stemming from the powerful engine: the large propeller necessary to cope with the power whirled a hefty weight of air around the fuselage and tail — making control more difficult. In an attempt to counter that effect, fuel was stored in the starboard float. Cooling the engine was another major concern, as indeed was always the case with the Spitfire. Radiators for this latest, S.5 racer, were integral with the exceptionally smooth wing surfaces. Construction showed a major change too, for, while the wings and tail were of wood, the fuselage and floats were of metal. Throughout design and research stages great was the care taken before three examples (*N219*, *N220* and *N222*) were built.

In the 1927 Race held at Venice the S.5s were flown by an RAF team, and to the delight of the British, Flight Lieutenant S.N.Webster in *N220* (fitted with an 875 hp Napier Lion engine) won at an average speed of 281.65 mph. Later in 1927 an S.5 achieved 319.57 mph, a British speed record. Only too well aware of the military potential of what was being achieved, the RAF decided to acquire the S.5s for research flying at Felixstowe. During an attempt to raise the speed record *N221* dived into the sea off Calshot on 12 March 1928, leaving the two remaining S.5s to join the High Speed Flight formed in June 1928 confirming — for the present — official interest in the race. Also observing the events was the large Vickers (Aviation) Ltd concern. Supermarine was a very small but a potentially very valuable company. In late 1928, Vickers acquired Supermarine which gave the smaller company a much better financial base, and the larger a highly talented team of designers and craftsmen.

The next race was set for September 1929 with Britain, the previous winner, hosting the event at Spithead. Again, the demand was for even more refined design — and how often was that to be true of the Spitfire? Equally, there was a need for far more power. Napier had concluded that their Lion engine was at the end of its feasible development and had no plans for a replacement. The Air Ministry stepped in and invited Rolls-Royce to develop an engine for the racers, unknowingly taking a step from which the spin-off would have enormous consequences. Indeed, it was to prove the stride, which more than any other single move, brought salvation to civilization. In November 1928 work began on the Rolls-Royce 'R' engine, an adaptation of the existing Rolls-Royce Buzzard (itself a scaled up Kestrel engine upon which the Merlin was based).

Tidied to fit the Supermarine Racer's airframe, fitted with a new special supercharger and running on special petrol, the 'R' engine produced 1,900 hp. The vital importance of power plant development was to be as important in the Spitfire story as it was to the racer. Calm, collected Mitchell must have been overcome with concealed excitement upon discovering that the engine reckoned likely to give 1,500 hp was already exceeding that output. The forecast 350 mph for the S.6 could now even become 400 mph which, in 1929, must have seemed phenomenal. Indeed, not until 1941 were fighters available possessing such speed.

But it was not only the speed of the metal-skinned S.6 which was high: weighing 4,500 lb loaded, due to its larger engine and bigger airframe (compared with the S.5's 3,250 lb) the S.6's rate of climb was reckoned likely to reach a handsome 5,000 fpm. A modified engine cowling was fitted, both floats now held fuel, and the forward float struts were repositioned. Making use of all available space the oil tank was, most unconventionally, fitted into the fin. But the most elaborate changes were required to suit the powerful new engine. Its operating temperature was extremely critical, so the cooling system had to be elaborate with oil circulating to the fin and back, passing through coolers under the fuselage.

Two S.6s, *N247* and *N248*, were officially ordered in 1929 with competition now provided by two Gloster VI seaplanes. By completion the S.6s were found to weigh over 5,000 lb — more than forecast — but the enormous torque effect from the engine was somewhat reduced when adjustment was made to the fuel load in the starboard tank. To combat insufficient engine cooling, radiators were skilfully incorporated in the floats, and wing-tip scoops were also fitted forcing air into the

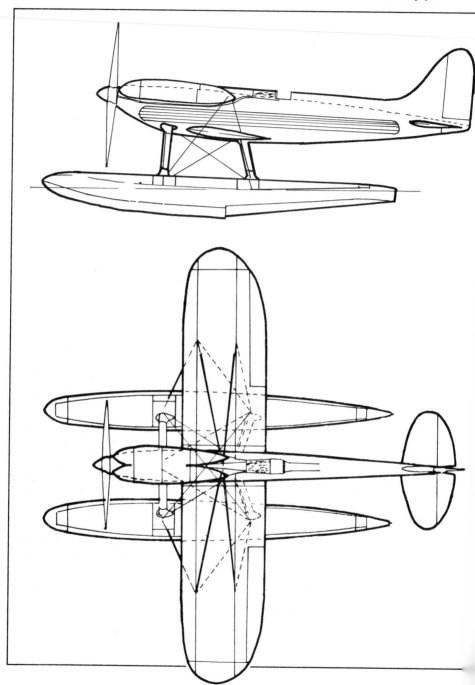

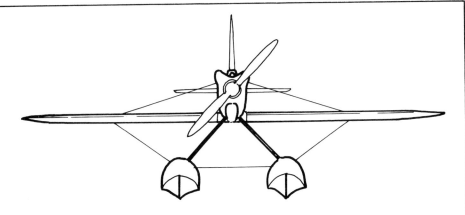

Layout of the Supermarine S6 series. Wing span 30 ft, wing chord 5 ft 8 in; overall length 28 ft 10 in; float track 7 ft 6 in.

Below *The beautiful lines of* N248, *the second S6, are evident here* (RAF Museum P015281).

wings to cool the radiators installed there. Every adjustment made, a process which continued up to the race, was liable to increase the weight. Soon weight had risen to 5,500 lb, thought likely to bring disappointment. Lessons learned in these critical weeks must surely have been of enormous value when the Spitfire was repeatedly refined, and especially when the powerful Griffon engine supplanted the Merlin.

A million people were at Calshot to watch the race which was flown on 7 September 1929. All went well and, flying *N247*, Flying Officer H. R. D. Waghorn won handsomely at 328.63 mph. Flying Officer Richard L. Atcherley, later of considerable wartime fame, captured two World Closed Circuit Speed Records, the 50 km at 332.49 mph and 100 km at 331.75 mph. Then on 12 September Squadron Leader A. H. Orlebar — who was later to play a major part in fighter development during his time at the Air Ministry — won the World Air Speed Record at 357.7 mph. September 1929 had proven indeed a stupendous month for the enterprising little Southampton firm. Could it now produce the outright winner of the Schneider Trophy?

With the Depression closing in, the Labour government confirmed support for the 1931 race only to withdraw it two months later. How much wiser it would have been to have funded the racer programme than to have squandered it on the ill-fated *R-101* politicians' airship! Beware all claims of all governments! In this case politicians maintained that the race had forsaken its prime purpose to become a sporting event — which was utterly untrue. Advancement of seaplane development remained its paramount purpose. Secondly, it was claimed that enough had already been learned about high-speed aircraft development, a monumentally idiotic pronouncement! Stating that, for those reasons, the expenditure involved was unjustified, the government announced that future race participation must be privately funded.

During December 1930 the Society of British Aircraft Constructors discussed the matter, and considered the racing of modified seaplanes. The cost of managing the project and organizing race participation quite apart from the expense of engine and airframe development and test flying, looked enormous. Regretfully it was decided that the uneasy economic climate prohibited such expenditure.

Within days all was rescued by a benefactor to whom the nation should forever be grateful. Highly patriotic, very flamboyant, wealthy Lady Houston — no friend of the Labour government — gave £100,000 for a British contender in the 1931 race. In actuality, she was giving far more than money. Lady Houston was making possible continued investigation into high-speed flight at a vital time for, very soon, R. J. Mitchell and his team would turn their attention to the creation of a fighter for the RAF.

With little more than six months in which to produce a 1931 racer, Supermarine decided to re-design the S.6. Slightly enlarged, it would be strengthened and skilfully braced. Additional fuel would be better distributed in the floats to further reduce increased torque expected from the revised Rolls-Royce 'R' engine driving a new propeller. The great attention to detail for which Mitchell and his team was now famous led to extensive wind tunnel and water tank tests. Flutter seemed

S1596, *the second Supermarine S6B* (RAF Museum P015278).

certain to increase as the aircraft's speed rose, and was reckoned likely to be due in part to inevitable slight inaccuracies in construction however much care was exercised. For more precise handling, tabs were added to control surfaces.

After much revision, *N247*, a reconditioned S.6 and called the S.6A, flew in June 1931 and was soon followed by a second 6A, *N248*. Then came the two newly built S.6Bs for the 1931 race, *S1595* and *S1596*. Meanwhile, changes to the rules meant that more fuel would need to be carried — which demanded even more power. To compensate, the floats were lengthened slightly and narrowed — changes which offered additional radiator space so that now half the entire surface of the aircraft was given over to cooling devices!

Mitchell had latterly asked for an engine capable of, or at least briefly giving, 2,300 hp, which meant supercharger and other modifications. Thus, the racer again was pointing the way in which the Spitfire would later be developed. The power now conferred upon the S.6B made handling on the water extremely difficult and, like modern combat aircraft, it flew with the aid of sheer brute force.

September 1931 was as vital to the Spitfire saga as that aeroplane's contribution to our survival became in September 1940. Whether the 1931 opposition concluded that they did not wish to be seen failing in the race against the British, we shall never know for certain: certainly time and the expense of the race were factors which deterred their entries, as were general technical developments and misfortunes. Whatever the reasons, only Britain entered the 1931 Schneider Trophy Race over the Solent, and at an average speed of 340.08 mph Flight Lieutenant John N. Boothman flying *S1595* won the Schneider Trophy outright for Britain. (The Trophy is still on public view in the South Kensington Science Museum.) Then, later the same day, Flight Lieutenant George Stainforth clinched the Absolute Speed Record, flying *S1596* at 379.05 mph. But there was clearly better capability left in the aircraft, and with an improved fuel mix *S1595* reached an amazing 407.5 mph and became the first aircraft in the world to exceed 400 mph in level flight. Such speeds were quite astonishing at the time and the question was how soon would they become commonplace?

It was one thing to devise high-speed one-off aeroplanes; it was another to finance their development. Inevitably, some government funding was essential and when in 1930 the Air Ministry announced its ideas for a new high-speed fighter for the RAF, Supermarine decided to show interest.

Chapter 4
A fighter is born

Fighters and their armament had barely changed since the 1914-18 War when, in the late 1920s, the Hawker Hart biplane day bomber gave a severe jolt to the RAF, for it possessed a performance as good as any current fighter's. Although the Bristol Bulldog was soon introduced, something far superior was needed.

Although money was short, the government agreed to Air Staff demands for an advanced fighter and in October 1931 the aircraft industry was told of a need for a 200 mph, four-gun fighter. Many unusual designs resulted, among them Mitchell's gull-winged Supermarine Type 224. Far from handsome, it was planned around a Rolls-Royce Goshawk engine, a relation to the plentiful Kestrel. Steam used to cool its running was to be condensed in the aircraft's wing leading edge, before returning as water to the engine cooling jacket. Schneider racers' influence upon the new aeroplane was evident. As a fighter though, the strange-looking Type 224 must have seemed a questionable starter.

The unusual gull wing was chosen in order to allow a large diameter propeller to be fitted: equally unusual were the giant fairings called 'trousers' each carrying a machine-gun and cloaking an undercarriage leg. But the Type 224 looked at least as good as other contenders and a prototype was ordered in June 1932, on the strength of Mitchell's speed forecast of 238 mph at 15,000 ft. Supermarine was a small firm, and had never produced aircraft in quantity. Therefore, in late 1932, the Air Ministry suggested that only a few of Mitchell's promising fighters be bought, to replace the handful of Hawker Furies employed to defend major ports.

In 1933 introduction of more potent 87 octane petrol enhanced prospects for engine development and then in March 1933 came radical suggestions for doubling the number of guns in fighters to eight. In the meantime Supermarine's fighter was progressing so slowly that the Air Ministry told the company that if the prototype did not reach Martlesham Heath for official tests by the end of 1933 it would be cancelled. Complications with the engine and attempts to reduce the weight were delaying the aircraft. A larger wing was devised to reduce the wing loading and it was 20 February 1934 before the aircraft flew. All along the Air Ministry believed that Mitchell was capable of better things, which was why it agreed to the machine proceeding. When it attained only 228 mph it was clear that the Type 224 could never answer the RAF's need. But as suspected, Supermarine had already been taking steps to produce something better.

By mid-1934, the demand for fighters with performance superior to anything so far even envisaged became obvious — aircraft able to fly 'as fast as possible' with rapid climb to about 20,000 ft were demanded, the likely height of future bombing raids undertaken above balloon barrages and anti-aircraft fire. in June 1934 it was decided to forsake the trusty old Vickers machine-gun and acquire the newer Colt-Browning, and to fit eight of them in each fighter.

So many guns could not be fitted in the fuselage. Most, possibly all, would have to be installed in the wings, thus calling for very high reliability but problems of feeding in the ammunition, and of preventing them from icing up at high altitudes could be foreseen. Space would be needed in the wings to accommodate not only the guns, but as much fuel as possible and the retracting undercarriage too. Wing flaps would be needed for steep, short take-off and for slowing the landing speed.

Spitfire standard construction

All-metal stressed skin with special attention to surface finish. Fuselage: Semi-monocoque basically formed by fifteen frames and four longerons. Two rear frames formed the fin spars; tailplane attached to these. Wing: Single box spar and flush-riveted, internally braced leading edge structure carrying wing torsion loads. Fabric-covered ailerons, elevators and rudder with trim tabs in tail surfaces. Split trailing edge flaps able to deflect to ninety degrees. Undercarriage mounted on rear of spar, retraction by hand pumping on early aircraft. Differential wheel brakes.

Now came a plan to build an eight-gun fighter to replace all the others, to reach at least 275 mph and climb very fast. The pilot within a closed canopy would have radio equipment and an oxygen supply. If the fighter took long to evolve, then its top speed would need to be at least 300 mph, even 350 mph.

Mitchell admitted to the Air Ministry in July 1934 that he had been designing a better fighter. By then the Air Ministry too had its new ideas. Mitchell's new fighter, based on the Type 224, had an enclosed cockpit and retractable undercarriage but did away with the the gull wing. With reduced wingspan, the new design was thought likely to be 30 mph faster than its forerunner. Perhaps most important of all, it was to be powered by the latest Rolls-Royce PV-12 engine. Mitchell claimed that a prototype could fly in early 1935, and reach 265 mph. But his fighter was unacceptable because of its four-gun armament. Higher speed, and eight guns firing in combined bursts of two seconds — a limitation caused by the speed of battle — were reckoned sufficient to destroy a raider. These the new fighter must have.

Fitting those eight guns posed a major problem. Thick wings like those of the new Hawker fighter, the forthcoming Hurricane, made that easier, and they could accommodate various other items. But, by greatly increasing drag, they reduced the performance.

During the second half of 1934, sandy-haired Mitchell — 'RJ' to his colleagues — and the Supermarine team pooled the knowledge they had won during the Schneider Trophy racing days and more latterly with the Type 224 in discussions

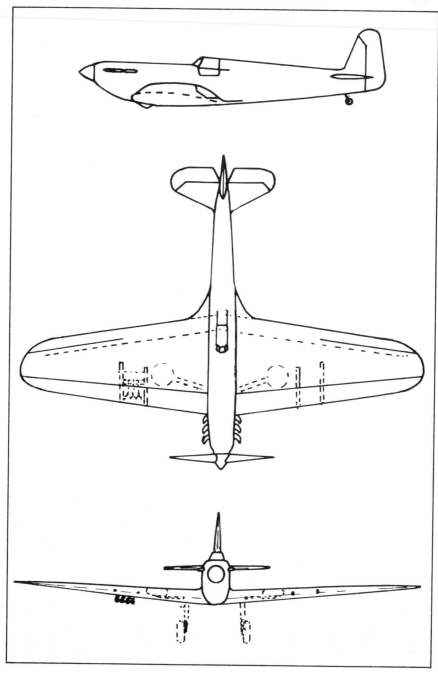

with the Air Ministry and the RAF. By late 1934 the fighter's cockpit canopy was merged into the fuselage top line, and four guns were situated in its wings. Then, on 6 November, the Vickers board gave the go-ahead for the construction of a company funded prototype, the Type 300, powered by a Rolls-Royce PV-12 — later known as the famous Merlin. The Air Ministry again reviewed the design and in December, and although it was still a four-gun fighter, decided to fund a prototype allocating £10,000 for what in January they designated the F.37/34.

Air Staff viewing of the wooden mock-up of the impressive Type 300 followed in April 1935. After discussing their plans for a 1940s fighter with Mitchell they concluded that his current design would probably perform as well as such an interceptor — but eight guns were essential. Eight guns could be achieved by increasing the chord and spreading the load to accommodate them, but fitting the additional four guns must reduce the fuel load. The design team soon came along with an imaginative answer, an elliptical plan wing. Such a design was not unique, for Heinkel, in Germany, had already used such wing planforms. For the Supermarine fighter the elliptical wing was an ideal solution. Not only did it offer good aerodynamic qualities, it also provided sufficient space for guns, undercarriage and cooling systems. For purposes of strength and loading, the guns were to be spaced along the wing.

Left *A stage in Spitfire development, based upon the F.7/30 projects, in which the rear fuselage depth is increased, the undercarriage simplified to reduce weight and the Goshawk engine retained. The four guns are all wing-mounted, each having 500 rounds of ammunition. Undercarriage track is 6 ft, the fuselage length is 27 ft 4 in and the mainplanes have equal leading and trailing edge taper.*

Below *Exciting indeed was the sight of* K5054 *as '2' in the New Types Park at the 1936 Hendon display.*

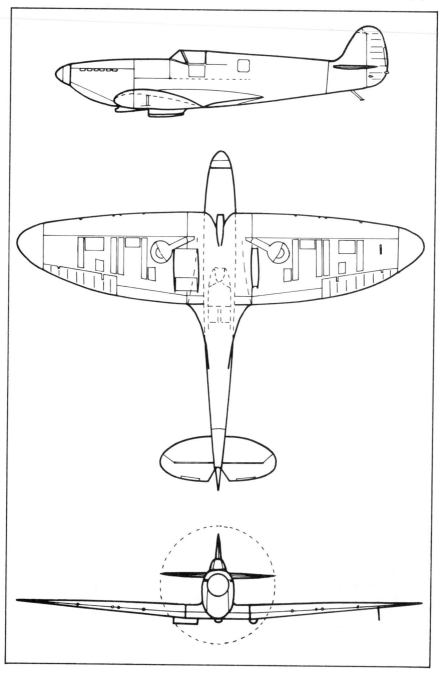

A thin wing, the smallest possible fuselage head-on section, minute attention to streamlining and the curves of the fuselage, all combined to produce not only a very fast fighter but one of the most elegant aircraft of all time. It was hoped that the prototype would fly in October 1935. Instead, it was the 'competing' Hurricane which flew first. Air Ministry records and indeed many others state that it was 5 March 1936 when the unpainted Supermarine prototype made its brief, first flight from Eastleigh, Southampton Airport, in the hands of Captain Mutt Summers. But Jeffrey Quill, so much associated with Spitfire testing, states in his book *A Test Pilot's Story* (John Murray) that on 6 March 1936 he flew Mutt Summers from Martlesham Heath to Eastleigh for him to fly the Spitfire for the first time on that day. What is certain is that it was an intimate, 'family' occasion, Summers using the short runway and finding the aircraft to handle well. After his fifteen-minute flight during which the undercarriage was not retracted, he was clearly extremely satisfied with *K5054*'s performance. He must surely have recognized that it was, from the start, a winner.

Mitchell was a highly talented, imaginative perfectionist. Little wonder then that he soon insisted that *K5054*, the Spitfire prototype, should be flying much faster. So far it had only reached 335 mph. The first attempt to raise the speed came with the fitting of a different propeller, which reduced the drag. As a result *K5054* reached 348 mph during testing by the company.

On 26 May 1936 the pale blue-grey prototype flew to Martlesham Heath for the all-important sampling of its capability by government and RAF test pilots. All were extremely impressed and commented upon the aircraft's effective and responsive controls. They thought the cockpit layout to be good, and found the aeroplane acceptably stable and without vices.

As a result of the glowing report, the Air Ministry ordered 300 examples of the Supermarine 16/36 (Merlin II engine) in June 1936. Of these, 270 were to be delivered by March 1939. The order would have been larger had not Hawker devised a fighter suitable for faster production than Supermarine's. Hawker also possessed far superior production resources and capability. Their fighter was easier to construct, more robust and had been devised with production in mind. Since the Rolls-Royce Merlin had been chosen for both types and was already earmarked for other aircraft, the Air Staff concluded that the Hawker fighter could be in service well before the other because of its less complex and less advanced design. Accordingly, 600 Hawker fighters were ordered, twice the number contracted for with Supermarine.

Powering the first prototype, *K5054*

Rolls-Royce Merlin C (early development engine of 990 hp initially fitted) exhausting into twelve ports flush with the fuselage. Drove a de Havilland two-blade fixed-pitch wooden propeller. Replaced by Merlin F (similar to Merlin Mk 1) of 1,035 hp and coupled to exhaust manifold. Later had a Merlin G (similar to Mk II) fitted with ejector exhausts which added about 10 mph to top speed.

Left *The Spitfire first prototype, K5054.*

Results of *K5054*'s initial, official tests at Martlesham Heath

Weight at take-off: 5,332 lb. Top speeds: 349 mph TAS at 16,800 ft, and 324 mph TAS at 30,000 ft: climb to 15,000 ft took 5 minutes 42 seconds, 30,000 ft reached in 17 minutes. Service ceiling 34,500 ft. Summary of Martlesham's conclusions: 'simple and easy to fly', 'has no vices', 'controls well harmonized', 'excellent compromise between manoeuvrability and steadiness for shooting', 'can be flown without risk by average fully-trained Service pilot'.

The Hawker Hurricane entered service eight months before the Spitfire. The Spitfire name, incidentally, had been applied by Supermarine to the unsuccessful Type 224. When the Vickers management used it in respect of the later design Mitchell strongly disapproved. Nevertheless, the name Spitfire was officially approved by the Air Council for service use on 28 July 1936. Between August and late 1936 the prototype was modified to take a later type Merlin F engine, radio, gunsight and its eight guns. During high altitude firing trials at Martlesham oil froze in the breeches of the guns, and necessary heating of the gun bays was achieved by leading in warm air. The system took some time to perfect.

Those close to R. J. Mitchell realized that by now the brilliant designer was a very sick man. In 1933, before starting work on the Spitfire, he had undergone a cancer operation. Three years later he was again suffering and this time there was to be no cure. He was flown abroad to obtain the best possible treatment, but to no avail. On 11 June 1937, at the early age of 42, one of the most able aircraft designers of all time died. For a small concern to which he had contributed vastly the loss must have been personally felt. There would however be an instant memorial and one which vast numbers of people would come to know and to admire enormously.

Of course, Mitchell had not worked alone. His team included others of considerable ability and particular skills, among them Joseph Smith. Joe Smith had served his apprenticeship with Austin and joined Supermarine in 1921 as senior draughtsman. In 1926 he became chief draughtsman and later took charge of the detail design of the Spitfire. His work had, in particular, centred upon the

---

The High Speed Spitfire

An idea was born in August 1937 for a Spitfire to snatch the world's landplane speed record. Two Merlin II engines using special fuel and accepting very high boost pressure were modified to briefly give 2,000 bhp. *K9834* was modified, its wing span being reduced to 33 ft 8 in and a revised cockpit cover fitted. Registered *N17*, it had an enlarged radiator (with additional coolant as an alternative) and a four-blade fixed pitch wooden propeller. Finish overall was high gloss blue with silver trim. First flown 10 November 1938, it reached 408 mph — insufficient to win the record lifted to 469.22 mph by an Me 209 in April 1939. Nevertheless, *N17* by its performance proved the Spitfire's enormous development potential. Fitted with a Merlin XII, it joined the PRU on 24 November 1940 serving as their communications aircraft throughout the war. Struck off charge 21 May 1946.

Spitfire's structure and he now became Supermarine's Chief Designer, a post he held throughout the Spitfire years.

A few weeks after Mitchell's death the prototype belly landed near Ipswich. When in September 1937 it emerged after repair, it had a Merlin II, and was wearing dark green and dark earth camouflage, its under surfaces being silver. Gone was the original pale blue-grey finish, for here was the prototype of a war machine. Spitfire production was already underway, but progressing painfully slowly. Tough official irritation was being forcefully expressed, but there was little that could be done to speed things. Supermarine had limited production facilities and only more contracts in earlier years could have altered that. Indeed, between 1919 and 1936 the company had built only 137 aeroplanes, the vast majority of which were Walrus amphibians. A small work force, limited factory space, shortage of local labour and a lack of production expertise due to small production runs, all combined to cause problems. The curvaceous lines of the Spitfire did not at first lend themselves to high speed production. Wings and tails were sub-contracted, their manufacturers complaining of unsuitable drawings from which to work. Unfamiliarity with the construction of metal components further aggravated things, and not until 14 May 1938 did the first production Spitfire, *K9787*, make its maiden flight — a year later than originally planned.

On 4 August 1938, No 19 (Fighter) Squadron stationed at Duxford in Cambridgeshire became the first to receive a Spitfire and soon commenced 400 hours of intensive flying to explore its full service capability. The arrival of that first Spitfire brought less euphoria than might be expected, partly because the eight-gun Hurricane had long been in service, and also because Supermarine was in official 'bad books' because of the production delays.

During the following autumn and winter 19 Squadron — and soon its companion, 66 Squadron — flew their Spitfires intensively, frequently demonstrating a twelve-aircraft air drill over Cambridgeshire. Duxford, a small grass airfield, came to be dominated by the unmistakable roar of the Merlin as many a pilot tried the RAF's fastest fighter, usually discovering in a do-it-yourself fashion how to fly the aircraft. A klaxon warned of the 'gear down' need as speed was reduced for landing. Disconnection, a tempting action, brought several moments of despair — and most ignominiously and publicly to one pilot during the 1939 Empire Air Day air race!

By the outbreak of war, when production had reached about one Spitfire a day, ten squadrons including three of the Auxiliary Air Force were flying Spitfires, of which 305 had been delivered — but 27 had already been struck off charge through accidents or other forms of 'wastage'.

Early Spitfire production

First production order for 310 examples placed in June 1936. Produced initially at Woolston and Itchen factories, aided by Folland, General Aircraft, Pobjoy and Westland as sub-contractors.

April 1938 : contract for 1,000 Spitfires to be built at Castle Bromwich Aircraft Factory.

14 May 1938: *K9787* first production Mk 1 made its first flight. By September 1939, 2,160 Spitfires on order.

As it slipped in over the South Coast, the first production Spitfire **K9787** *must have delighted Charles Brown when he took this memorable picture* (RAF Museum 5784–6).

Ah! the joy of the sight of 'Air Drill by 19 Squadron'. In 1939 it was almost a daily feature over Cambridgeshire (RAF Museum 5838–5).

In the summer months of 1939 Duxford took on a very sombre warlike appearance with its Spitfires toned down in camouflage. Sandbags surrounded many buildings, gun positions were built around the landing ground and ammunition was loaded ready for use. Everywhere there was a menacing atmosphere, a sense of certainty that conflict was imminent. Come the invasion of Poland and Spitfires of the three squadrons, Nos 19, 66 and 611 on detachment, were dispersed around the airfield boundary. The worst had come.

The first Spitfires for the Few

K9787 type trials, Martlesham July 1938. Radio trials Farnborough April 1939, converted for photo-reconnaissance with the PRU. Posted missing 30 June 1941.

K9788 Rolls-Royce and Martlesham trials July 1938. Re-engined with RM 3S February 1939 for Rolls-Royce trials: converted to Mk Va, despatched to Middle East and struck off charge 27 July 1944.

K9789 joined 19 Squadron 4 August 1938. Returned to Supermarine for examination 22 April 1939. With 65 Squadron 27 August 1940 to 28 November 1940: later used by 57 OTU, then 61 OTU, became *3594M*.

K9790 to 19 Squadron 11 August 1938. Returned to Supermarine for examination 6 May 1939. To 7 OTU in 1940: crash landed on 15 July 1940.

K9791 used by Supermarine as a trials and development aircraft from October 1938. To Photographic Development Unit 4 June 1940: missing on training flight 17 August 1940.

K9792 delivered to Duxford for 19 Squadron 29 July 1938: crash landed 20 September 1938 and written off 3 November 1938.

K9793 to Martlesham 9 September 1938 for equipment trials. To Supermarine for DH propeller tests 1 December 1938: to Martlesham to test propeller 24 January 1939. To RAE 18 July 1940; to 8 MU 19 August 1940; and to 92 Squadron 1 September 1940: written off 11 September 1940 due to battle damage.

K9794 to 19 Squadron 4 October 1938; crash landed Duxford 10 January 1939 and written off.

K9795 to 19 Squadron 27 September 1938. With 64 Squadron 20 April 1940–July 1940. To 603 Squadron 28 September 1940. With 222 Squadron 14 October–21 October 1940. Later served with 58 OTU, became *2867M* in January 1942.

K9796 With 19 Squadron 3 October 1938–21 November 1939. Later used by RAE: struck off charge 30 April 1945.

The pre-war RAF Squadrons — first deliveries

19 Squadron, Duxford, identity letters *WZ:* eg, *K9792* 29 July 1938
66 Squadron, Duxford, identity letters *RB:* eg, *K9802* 31 October 1938
41 Squadron, Catterick, identity letters *PN:* eg, *K9831-32* 30 December 1938
74 Squadron, Hornchurch, identity letters *JH:* eg, *K9860-63* 13 February 1939
54 Squadron, Hornchurch, identity letters *DL:* eg, *K9880-81* 2 March 1939
65 Squadron, Hornchurch, identity letters *FZ:* eg, *K9903* 21 March 1939
72 Squadron, Church Fenton, identity letters *SD:* eg, *K9922-25* 11 April 1939
602 Squadron, Abbotsinch, identity letters *ZT/LO:* eg, *K9962-63* 8 May 1939
611 Squadron, Speke, identity letters *GZ:* eg, *K9980* 18 May 1939
609 Squadron, Yeadon, identity letters *BL?:* eg, *L1081-82* 19 August 1939

Chapter 5
'Action Stations!'

Of 182 Spitfires distributed between ten squadrons, 150 were serviceable and ready for action when the war broke out on 3 September 1939. There were 203 pilots available to fly the Spitfires which equipped a third of Fighter Command's operational single-seat fighter squadrons. In all these squadrons held 570 aircraft. They were all waiting to repel an attack which never came. Such enemy probing as took place concerned East Coast shipping routes. Not until 16 October 1939 did the enemy attack the mainland — Ju 88s of KG 30 attempting to sink naval ships off Rosyth. Six Spitfires of 602 and 603 Squadrons raced into action, three pilots of the latter despatching a raider into the sea off Port Seton and thereby achieving the first Spitfire kill. No 602 Squadron followed suit with their first victory, another Ju 88 which crashed into the sea off Crail. Less satisfactory was the first loss of a Spitfire during an operational sortie, the misfortune befalling 41 Squadron, off the Yorkshire coast.

After several false alarms a confirmed Heinkel He 111 was discovered to have crossed the Sussex coast around midday on 20 November 1939 and turned north-east heading towards London. Spitfires and Hurricanes were ordered to intercept and eventually three Spitfires of 74 Squadron damaged it so seriously that it crashed off the East Anglian coast. Such events were rare and not until May 1940 was there much trade for the home-based fighters.

By then the development of the Spitfire and suitable engines for it were well under way. At the start of the war Rolls-Royce established a new team to tailor their latest engine, the 1,700 hp Griffon, to fit a 'Spitfire Mk II' increasing its speed to 400 mph. Being about 850 lb heavier than the Merlin, it needed a stronger airframe and for this reason the programme had to be shelved for the present. To interrupt the Merlin line and its production was far too dangerous at this stage of the war.

Rolls-Royce was also developing the two-stage blower 1,240 hp Merlin XX, and this Supermarine wedded to the Spitfire, producing the Mk III. Prior to its first flight in March 1940, its top speed was forecast as 390 mph at 21,000 feet and improved climb performance was expected. Enlarged radiators were needed as was a stronger wing spar, and being heavier, the aircraft's performance did not reach expectations. Supermarine planned to fit four cannon to the Mk III Spitfire, and to improve its rate of roll the Mk III's wing tips were clipped to 30 ft

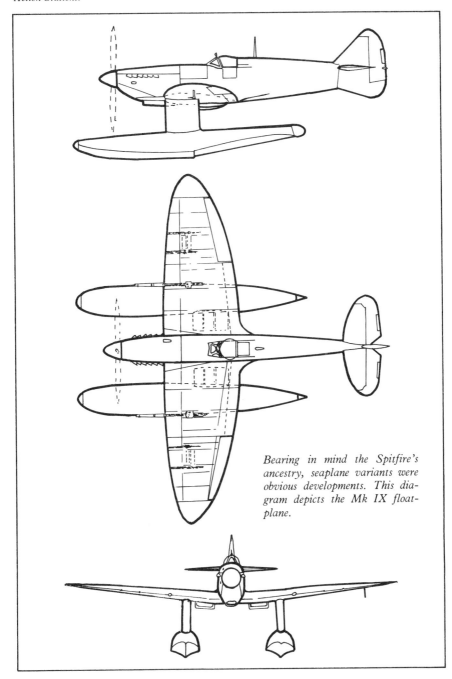

Bearing in mind the Spitfire's ancestry, seaplane variants were obvious developments. This diagram depicts the Mk IX floatplane.

6 in, spoiling its high altitude performance which the Merlin XX had been designed to improve.

Throughout the Spitfire's development, even the slightest changes could have a major effect upon handling and performance. Always, the gains needed to be set against loss. That was strongly the Air Staff view for although on 12 December 1939 they decided that the development of the Spitfire must have priority over that of the Hurricane, they concluded that the Merlin XX would best be used improving the latter. January 1940 brought first thoughts of extending the Spitfire's duration but this was far easier to achieve with the Hurricane whose thick wing allowed ample space for attachment points for long range tanks and later bombs and rockets. For that reason it served overseas sooner than the Spitfire.

When war engulfed Norway in April 1940, and British forces were despatched to the scene, there came a hasty demand for Spitfires to be fitted with floats. Supermarine rapidly devised a conversion and at the same time planned a Mk III floatplane. Although a mixture of Spitfire seaplanes was produced, they saw limited service, and only in the Mediterranean Theatre.

Undoubtedly the most important advances which could overtake the Spitfire concerned the fitting of improved powerplants. Early investigations also showed that superior propellers could bring most useful advances. The first Spitfires had huge, two-bladed, very solid, wooden Watts propellers, but already available were propellers whose blade pitch, or angle at which they snatched at the air, could be

A variety of schemes for Spitfire floatplanes were prepared. Illustrated is LF Mk IXb MJ892. At least eight floatplane Spitfires were produced (IWM).

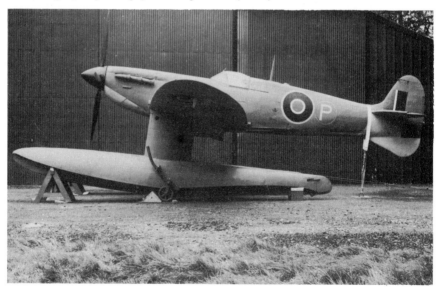

Dispersed between bell tents, an 'acc starter' and a Zwicky refuelling bowser, Spitfires of 611 Squadron photographed about May 1940 (RAF Museum P015053).

changed. Two settings were possible and such 'variable pitch', three-bladed propellers were introduced onto Spitfires before the war. In effect such propellers had one setting for low speeds and another for high speeds — interim speeds being poorly catered for. Now came the rather misleadingly named 'constant speed' propeller: by means of a governor the pitch setting could now be related to the entire speed range. That would bring great benefits to performance, although it meant aircraft being withdrawn for modifications.

June 1940 was to see the start of the programme, but by then the situation across the Channel had become perilous and the fitting of constant speed propellers was delayed by a few weeks. High over French beaches, largely unseen from the ground, Spitfire squadrons flew thousands of sorties, protecting the withdrawal of the Expeditionary Force. The large scale enemy attacks directed against the little ships at Dunkirk and valuable naval units in the Channel also met fierce response from the Spitfires. Within a few days much of the Spitfire force had faced the foe and had been moved to forward bases. The intensity of the fighting is rarely recounted, probably because it was so soon overshadowed. Worse, far, far worse was about to engulf the Spitfire squadrons.

Chapter 6
Most fateful days

'What General Weygand called the Battle of France is over', said Mr Churchill, 'I expect that the Battle of Britain is about to begin.' It was fortunate that siren voices discouraging re-armament had been silenced sufficiently to enable the Hurricane and Spitfire to materialize just in time to save us. Alarmingly, the wisdom of a policy combining highly powerful defence capabilities with a readiness to extend a friendly hand is a lesson which still has not been learned, yet it is one that all history proclaims — and loudly.

When that ferocious conflict which came to be called the Battle of Britain began it is impossible to decide. It may be reckoned as starting in late May 1940 when the Luftwaffe began bombing Britain by night or when RAF bombers started formation attacks on German bomber bases, or on 3 July 1940 when the Luftwaffe first mounted daylight attacks along our eastern seaboard. Official historians chose 10 July, when formations of raiders attacked Channel shipping. What is indisputable is that the Spitfire was the Luftwaffe's most admired and feared British fighter of those times.

A respite of about six weeks came between the evacuation of British troops from Dunkirk and the Luftwaffe's onslaught on Britain. German forecasts were that it would take about a month to destroy the RAF and allow an invasion of England to take place. Air Chief Marshal Sir Hugh Dowding had held his Spitfires back from being wasted over France, and operating in conditions for which they were not designed. While Hurricane squadrons fought in France, displaying high courage and enduring enormous losses, Spitfire squadrons began to congregate on bases in the east and south-east of England to afford high cover to the troop evacuations from Dunkirk and other French ports, guard our ships and patrol over our ports. Many Hurricane and Spitfire pilots flew several operational sorties daily during that period of intense activity, fought many battles and welcomed the respite which ensued after the fall of France.

While the Luftwaffe organized itself for its great onslaught upon Britain it mounted night operational training sorties. Although the Spitfire was theoretically a day and night fighter it was not really suitable for the second role. Nevertheless, late on 18 June 1940, No 19 Squadron which had fought over Dunkirk was ordered to intercept Heinkel 111s attempting to bomb airfields and rail targets in East Anglia. Rather unexpectedly, Flying Officer Petra spotted a

Spitfire Mk 19 PM631 *of the Battle of Britain Flight in the markings of No 74 Squadron before being repainted in 610 Squadron colours* (Stuart Howe).

Above *Supermarine S 6B S1595, the 1931 Schneider Trophy competitor now preserved in London's Science Museum, with the Trophy itself in the foreground.*

Below *Rolls-Royce Merlin 60 series engine also preserved in the Science Museum.*

Above *The Battle of Britain Flight's proudest machine, a genuine Battle of Britain Mk IIa, P7350, here erroneously marked as a 266 Squadron machine before it was repainted.*

Below *Spitfire Vb AB910 fitted with a Merlin 32 engine and four-bladed propeller following the accident with a Harvard in Switzerland.*

Spitfires over the Cambridgeshire countryside during the making of The Battle of Britain film in the 1960s. In the centre of the trio is the two-seater Mk 9 used as a camera aircraft (Spitfire Productions Ltd).

moonlit Heinkel 111. To assist his aim and that of a nearby Blenheim crew he switched on his landing light. As he fired so did the Heinkel's rear gunner, as a result of which both aircraft crashed in flames — Petra survived, badly burned, and the Spitfire had made its first night kill.

On 10 July, the official opening date of the Battle of Britain, Fighter Command held nineteen Spitfire and 38 Hurricane squadrons and during the Battle the average front line squadron daily strength was 465 Hurricanes and 290 Spitfires. Hurricanes were at all times numerically greater. Within the four months of the campaign 628 Spitfires and 1,025 Hurricanes were built, and by October output of both types was about equal. Post-war official analysis showed that Spitfires shot down about half the total number of enemy aircraft destroyed, including considerably more Bf 109 fighters than were shot down by Hurricanes.

Forecasts of the way in which the Luftwaffe would attack Britain did not usually assume that enemy bombers would operate at short range and have strong fighter cover. Nevertheless, because the Luftwaffe flew from bases just across the Channel, formations heading for England could be observed as they assembled — which allowed fighter squadrons to prepare to intercept. The Luftwaffe was largely a tactical air force. Its application in a semi-strategic role placed it at a disadvantage as it faced Fighter Command, precisely organized and trained to meet the coming threat.

Average top speed of a Hurricane at this time was about 310 mph at 17,000 ft, that of a Spitfire about 350 mph at 18,500. Because of that difference in performance and superior agility, Spitfires were more often directed against high flying German fighters than bombers, but in a melee both British types fought for any kill. Morale in Fighter Command was very high despite the grim situation, and pilots defending their home land naturally fought vigorously, bravely supported by Allies from overrun nations. The RAF was also, fortunately, led by long-serving experienced senior officers and, unlike the Luftwaffe, had known an uninterrupted existence since 1918.

Early stages of the Battle found the enemy coming in at around 16,000 ft. As the action proceeded and the strength of enemy fighter cover increased, the fighting height rose to over 20,000 ft — which favoured the Spitfire. For every fighter pilot there were basic combat rules to follow, for survival: watch for the enemy

---

Spitfire 1 — salient data and performance

1 Prototype — top speed 349 mph at 16,800 ft, maximum cruise speed 311 mph at 15,000 ft, time to 15,000 ft was 5.7 minutes. Time to 30,000 ft was 17 minutes and service ceiling, 34,500 ft. Fully loaded take-off weight, 5,332 lb. 2 Production aircraft — K9787 (Merlin II, normal bhp 966, rated altitude 12,250 ft). Wing span 36 ft 10 in. Length overall 29 ft 9 in. Height over prop 12 ft 3 in, minimum height 8 ft 10 in. Track 6 ft.

Total weight (fully loaded) 5,819 lb. Total fuel 84 gallons, oil 5.5 gallons. Maximum speed 362.5 mph at 18,500 ft, take-off untouch speed 86 mph. Best rate of climb 2,530 fpm at 11,000 ft (reached in 4.8 minutes), reached 20,000 ft in 9.4 minutes, service ceiling (31,900 ft) in 31.7 minutes. Touch down speed 60 mph. Take-off run to clear 50 ft, 720 yd. Landing run, using brakes, 315 yd.

> ## Typical Spitfire 1
> Merlin III of summer 1940, three-blade 10 ft 9 in diameter Rotol propeller. Wing span 36 ft 10 in. Length 29 ft 11 in. Loaded weight 6,050 lb, took 370 yd to take off over 50 ft, braked landing run 310 yd (with wooden propeller took 420 yd to take off, 380 yd for landing). Top speeds — 320.5 mph at 10,000 ft, 353.5 mph at 20,000 ft, 319 mph at 30,000 ft. Service ceiling 34,700 ft. Climb rates, to 10,000 ft 3.5 minutes 20,000 ft in 7.7 minutes, 30,000 ft in 16.4 minutes.

attacking out of the sun; never follow the foe down following a lucky strike, or for too long; operate with the pack, never alone; close in before firing; and at all times keep an eagle eye on as much of the battle as possible.

To a large extent both British fighters were well suited to the fight, although in a very fast dive the Spitfire's ailerons were difficult to control. Spitfire cockpit canopy tops were generally humped, but the rear view was still not good. A mirror attachment was needed but the modification reduced the top speed by about 7 mph. Small though that seems, the Bf 109 and Spitfire were so closely matched that the slightest advantage was valuable. Canopy side panels came in for criticism because they were not optically flat. Should they mist over, or be none too clean, then it could mean that a pilot might not see the distant foe in time. Superior, bulged side panels were introduced in 1940. Slight oil leaks could coat the canopy, but a more frequent problem arose when steam was ejected after glycol boiled during combat and then froze on the windscreen, prone also to freezing condensation.

High speed combat was so costly on fuel that a normal sortie could last for little more than an hour, after which refuelling and re-arming averaged about fifteen minutes — if there were no snags, no simple damages to attend to. Longer breaks were usual, squadrons tending to fly about three interceptions a day. With their aircraft in vics of three, stepped in line astern, they adopted a formation permitting the wing men to peel away easily to follow the leader.

For a while it seemed that the cannon-armed Messerschmitt Bf 109E might possess advantages over the Spitfire, but its controls were heavier. The Spitfire had a tighter turning circle, faster climb and usually superior speed making it a superb dog-fighter which frequently out-performed its rival. However, often-quoted performance figures for these fighters were achieved during scientifically measured test flights and never in the vastly different conditions of combat. The Spitfire pilot was usually trained for just the task that he was performing: the pedigree of his foes suited them better to a different battle style. The enemy's main advantage lay in numerical superiority, although he was fighting over enemy territory, with all the disadvantages that held.

One of the heaviest blows to the Spitfire came with the destruction of its Southampton factories, Itchen being raided twice, on 24 September by Messerschmitt Bf 110 fighter-bombers and on 26 September when the Woolston Works was also smashed by a textbook carpet bombing raid by Heinkel He 111s of KG 55 — all of which cost the lives of 135 Supermarine workers. Fortunately some dispersal of construction had taken place prior to the raid, Spitfire parts already being made at Southampton University, in hotels and large houses, but the Ministry of Aircraft Production wanted wider production distribution. The 'Southern Region' was established with its design and administration centre at Hursley Park near Winchester. Over 10,000 workers were soon employed, about half of them women. Five production centres were later set up, and seven airfields (Aldermaston, Chattis Hill, Chilbolton, Eastleigh, Henley, Keevil, and Worthy Down) eventually became available for flight testing. Although the Luftwaffe tried to cripple the huge Castle Bromwich works in 1940, they escaped fairly lightly.

If 3 July can be called the start of the Battle of Britain, then the first confirmed Spitfire victories in the campaign fell to 603 Squadron, three of whose pilots had confirmed victories on that day. All were Ju 88s brought down off Montrose, Peterhead and Stonehaven. No 616 Squadron was awarded a possible Do 17 off Yorkshire while 54 Squadron's engagement of Do 17s attempting to attack Manston opened the Spitfire fighting over south-east England, traditional Battle of Britain country. The first Spitfire to be lost during the Battle was *K9928*, victim of a lightning strike near Margate which resulted in the death of its pilot, Sergeant White.

Of the Spitfire squadrons, Nos 54, 65 and 74 Squadrons found themselves involved most in the fighting as the ferocious combat began. To their cost, 54 and 65 were 'bounced' from above by Bf 109s on 7 July, over Deal and Folkestone respectively, five Spitfires being destroyed. How essential in combat was the advantage of height. ... Frequently these squadrons faced early morning and evening 'sweeps', flown by Bf 109s in large numbers probing and tempting Britain's fighter defences. This led to fierce fights in which the Spitfires increasingly excelled despite their attackers' numerical superiority. One false move and the result of an engagement was certain disaster.

The tempo of air combat was indeed high. Famous Al Deere was flying Spitfire *P9398* over Manston on 9 July when he collided head-on with a Bf 109, a disaster from which he was very fortunate to escape. In a skirmish close by 54 Squadron lost three Spitfires, but the losses were far from one-sided for between 3 and 9 July at least nineteen enemy aircraft fell to Spitfire guns. Further west Spitfires based at Middle Wallop assisted in the protection of Portland harbour and on 11 July,

A comparison of available fighters in front line squadron service					
	10 Group	11 Group	12 Group	13 Group	*Total*
1 July 1940 (09:00)	— —	283 Hurricanes 128 Spitfires	48 Hurricanes 72 Spitfires	128 Hurricanes 92 Spitfires	459 292
1 August 1940 (09:00)	50 Hurricanes 63 Spitfire	216 Hurricanes 96 Spitfires	51 Hurricanes 61 Spitfires	149 Hurricanes 75 Spitfires	466 295
1 September 1940 (09:00)	61 Hurricanes 65 Spitfires	219 Hurricanes 97 Spitfires	62 Hurricanes 77 Spitfires	133 Hurricanes 46 Spitfires	475 285

when Ju 87s attacked an off-shore convoy, 609 Squadron fought the covering Bf 109s, a skirmish which cost the defenders two aircraft. As July unfolded it was mainly the Spitfires of 54, 65, 74, 602 and 603 Squadrons that were most heavily involved.

Attempting to reduce losses caused by enemy fighters unexpectedly getting onto a Spitfire's tail, 152 Squadron tried a new idea which was to lead to a major change in fighter tactics. Spitfires would regularly come to fight in pairs, so that the 'leader' would have his tail covered while both constantly weaved. Standard though the manoeuvre became, it was largely a post-Battle of Britain feature.

All the time the enemy was increasing the intensity of his campaign. Over north Kent on 24 July, 54, 65 and 610 Squadrons had a particularly fierce combat during which they shot down six Bf 109s. Another noteworthy attack developed on the afternoon of 25 July when Ju 88s of KG 51 covered by Bf 109s attacked Channel shipping. That led to one of the fiercest battles so far, with Spitfires destroying six enemy aircraft in a very tough fight but losing five of their number in the process.

The next major dog fight took place over Dover on the afternoon of 28 July when South African Squadron Leader 'Sailor' Malan led 74 Squadron, which was scrambled from Manston, into a ferocious fight with the Bf 109s of famous Major Werner Mölders' JG 51. While Hurricanes fought the bomber formation the dozen Spitfires brilliantly outfought the Germans losing two of their own number and destroying five Bf 109s. A further two Messerschmitts were badly damaged, one of them Molders' which crash landed in the Pas de Calais. Perhaps he neither gave, nor heeded in time, the famous warning cry *'Achtung, Spitfire'*.

Although much of the fighting took place over Kent, Sussex and the English Channel, east coast convoys were subjected to frequent enemy interest. Spitfires of 12 Group were brought into action, and these also faced single probing aircraft, raids upon airfields and high flying reconnaissance aircraft. In July 1940 about fifty enemy aircraft fell to Spitfire guns, about 65 to the Hurricane force.

The start of August found the Spitfires engaging ever more raiders over south-east England. Early morning 'sweeps' by Bf 109s still taunted 54, 64, 65 and 74 Squadrons into fast, furious dogfights while to the west 609 Squadron found itself repelling attacks by enemy aircraft on British shipping — at least before the really heavy daylight raids began.

During the last week of July 1940 the Germans planned the big attack *Adlerangriff* — the Eagle Attack. On 2 August detailed orders were issued, for the destruction of the Royal Air Force — within a few days — in an assault to commence on 10 August. A trifle late, the Luftwaffe launched its onslaught. On 12 August coastal targets came under sharp attack in half a dozen raids which involved hundreds of aircraft. Perhaps worst of all, bombing was carried out simultaneously on well spaced targets. As intended, the offensive brought the heaviest day's fighting so far as the Germans attempted to pave the way for crushing attacks to come.

Action for the Spitfire force started when Bf 109s of JG 52 made an early patrol over Kent and twelve Spitfires of 610 Squadron challenged them. Then came Bf 110s to attack radar stations in Kent and Sussex, and the airfields of Hawkinge and

Lympne. Ju 87s bombing a convoy were engaged by 65 Squadron's Spitfires, before a heavy attack developed on Portsmouth with some of the Ju 88s involved being detached to bomb Ventnor radar station. Four dozen Hurricanes intervened, along with Spitfires of 152 and 609 Squadrons. Over the Isle of Wight the Spitfires tackled the German fighter top cover in the most important engagement of the Battle so far. By the end of the day five radar stations had been damaged, that at Ventnor being unable to resume its role until 23 August. Operations on 12 August cost the Luftwaffe 36 aircraft shot down for an RAF loss of 22 fighters. Prior to the Portsmouth raid 65 Squadron had been bombed on the ground at Manston. Too late to protect the easy coastal target, its Spitfire defenders were trying to take off as bombs from KG 2's Dornier 17s fell around them.

Next day the Luftwaffe again attempted to split the British defence force, sought for evidence that the radar chain was broken and attacked airfields. Another 47 German aircraft were shot down, this time at a cost of thirteen British fighters. After dark, bombs, which did little damage, were directed at the Castle Bromwich Spitfire works. The Germans, meanwhile, were crediting themselves with far more success than they had so far achieved.

Very effective results were often obtained by but a few bombers and precision attacks were often more successful than a swarm of aircraft endulging in carpet bombing. At Middle Wallop on 14 August three He 111s of KG 55 raided the station highly effectively, delivering a devastating blow against a hangar. Spitfires of 609 Squadron, scrambled fast, caught up with the raiders and shot down the leader in a spectacular dogfight. But compared with what was to follow next day, this was as nothing. Its scale was hitherto unseen and the heaviest of the entire Battle.

Three *Luftflotten* were ordered to operate in daylight against Britain. Three groups were to tackle the south-east including fighters operating offshore, Heinkel 111s from Norway would make a surprise flanking raid on Tyneside and Ju 88s would attempt to neutralize the fighter stations at Church Fenton and Leconfield in Yorkshire. That, the Luftwaffe decided, would really give the British something to think about. Quickly following could be heavy bombing of factories by the Medway and a sneak raid upon Martlesham aerodrome in Suffolk. Two hours later seven formations would operate over Hampshire and Dorset before, at around 18:15 hours, airfields at Croydon and Middle Wallop would, hopefully, be destroyed. Hermann Göring, in his order of the day, reminded his crews that the main target was the RAF against which about 1,790 sorties were to be flown, 1,270 of them by fighters — which shows the healthy respect for Hurricanes and Spitfires which the enemy had already developed. Such respect was undoubtedly enhanced by the result of the day's fighting.

It was at around mid-morning on 15 August that radar stations first discovered intense enemy activity over the Pas de Calais. Ju 87 Stuka dive-bombers with Bf 109s above came in to attack Hawkinge and Lympne. Hurricanes of 501 Squadron and Spitfires of No 54 responded but, before they were in position to engage, Bf 109s swept down upon them destroying two of each squadron. The Norwegian

Rapid turn-round for 'PR:J' of 609 Squadron at Middle Wallop in August 1940.

Spitfire 'PR:Q' of 609 Squadron in a sandbag revetment at Middle Wallop, ready and waiting, in August 1940.

bomber force, He 111s of KG 26 from Stavanger escorted by Bf 110s, was already on a course which would take them to the Farne Islands. Spitfires were scrambled and tackled the escorting Bf 110s, 72 Squadron claiming two of the intruders and generally helping to break up the operation by finishing off three He 111s. But the northern probe was far from over for fifty Ju 88s of KG 30 were heading for the two fighter stations. Now it was the turn of 616 Squadron's Spitfires and Hurricanes of 73 Squadron to do battle. Seven bombers were shot down, three later crashed, and bombs fell wide — on the Whitley bomber base of Driffield. Not a very impressive effort, for sure.

Mid-afternoon brought the unexpected sneak raid by very low flying Bf 110 fighter-bombers on Martlesham, but the main attacks were directed on Eastchurch and Rochester which 64 Squadron's Spitfires were unable to divert. Later came the dive bombing of Portland harbour by Ju 87s and this time 234 Squadron's Spitfires tore into the protecting enemy fighters destroying three and causing another to crash in France.

By the end of the day a claim that 182 enemy aircraft had been destroyed was broadcast, and it arose in all sincerity from the intensive, confused nature of the

Spitfires known to have been in squadron hands on 15 August, 1940

19 Squadron: *R6761, R6770, R6776, R6809, R6889, R6911, R6912, R6923, R6958*

41 Squadron: *K9890, N3098, N3123, N3126, N3162, P9428, P9430, R6604, R6605, R6611, R6612, R6635, R6756, R6885, R6887*

54 Squadron: *L1042, N3097*, N3110, N3176, P9389, R6708, R6709, R6814, R6815, R6892, R6893, R6895, R6898, R6899, R6981*, R7015*, R7017, R7019, R7021, X4019, X4022, X4163*

64 Squadron: *K9805, K9964*, L1038, L1073, N3230, N3247, N3293, P9369, P9447, P9450, P9554, P9564, R6639, R6683, R6700, R6813, R6975, R6990*, X4067*

65 Squadron: *K9905, K9915, N3101, N3163, N3164, R6610, R6618, R6620, R6713, R6714, R6766, R6775, R6777, R6799, R6803, R6882, R6883*

66 Squadron: *K9823, K9944, N3029, N3032, N3035, N3044, N3048, N3049, N3121, N3182, N3225, R6689, R6715, R6800, X4020*

72 Squadron: *K9922, K9929, K9935, K9938, K9940, K9958, K9959, L1056, N3221, P9338, P9438, P9457, P9460, P9548, R6916, R6928, R6984, X4034, X4109*

74 Squadron: *K9871, K9951, K9953, L1089, P9492, R6716, R6759, R6772, R6773, R6780, R6839, R6840, X4024, X4027, X4068, X4069, X4101*

92 Squadron: *L1080, N3040, N3193, N3248, N3249, N3285, P9316, P9513, P9548, R6596, R6616, R6622, R6624, R6703, R6760*

152 Squadron: *K9900, K9930, K9954*, K9982, L1072, P7286* (Mk II), *R6608, R6763, R6764, R6810, R6829, R6897, X4017, X4171*

* Spitfires written off during the day.

222 Squadron: *K9826, K9962, L1010, N3233, P9323, P9324, P9325, P9326, P9337, P9360, P9361, P9362, P9364, P9378, P9397, P9469, R6628, R6719*

234 Squadron: *N3191, N3239, N3242, N3277, N3278, N3279, N3280, P9466, P9468, R6896, R6967, R6985, R6988*, X4016, X4023*

266 Squadron: *K9864, L1043, L1059, L1088, N3095, N3118, N3127, N3168*, N3178, N3181, N3189*, N3240, N3245, P9312, R6762, R6768, R6881, R6920, X4030, X4063*

602 Squadron: *K9839, K9910, K9955, K9969, L1002, L1004, L1019*, L1027, L1040, N3109, N3119, N3198, N3226, N3227, N3228, P9381, P9423, P9463, X4169*

603 Squadron: *L1021, L1024, L1046, L1067, L1070, N3056, N3105, N3267, N3288, P9459, R6626, R6717, R6721, R6751, R6752, R6753, R6808, R6835, R6836, R6989*

609 Squadron: *K9997, L1065, L1082, L1096, N3223, R6690, R6691, R6692, R6699, R6769, R6801, R6915, R6961, R6977, R6979, R6986*

610 Squadron: *K9931, K9960, L1009, N3284, P9496, P9498, P9545, R6595, R6621, R6641, R6694, R6695, R6802, R6806, R6891, R6976, R6993, X4065, X4070, X4102, X4103, X4105, X4168*

611 Squadron: *K9963, K9981, N3051, N3052, N3059, N3060, N3061, N3065, N3066, N3067, N3068, N3070, N3072, N3093, R6884, R6921, R6922, R6965, R6978, X4015* and Mk II: *P7291, P7292, P7302, P7303, P7304, P7305, P7314* assigned on 14 August, possibly not yet acquired

616 Squadron: *K9803, K9807, K9819, K9827, K9947, L1012, L1034, L1036, N3275, R6632, R6633, R6698, R6701, R6704, R6778, R6963, R6966, R6980, R7018*

fighting which cost the RAF nine Spitfires and eighteen Hurricanes. Spitfires certainly destroyed eight enemy aircraft, Hurricanes nineteen. As to precise victories over other Luftwaffe machines there is no certain knowledge, but in all at least 67 were brought down in combat.

There was no time to rest upon laurels, for on 16 August the Luftwaffe mounted three great assaults, firstly against Kent and the Thames Estuary, then against targets in Sussex and Hampshire and in the evening raids were despatched to four points between Harwich and the Isle of Wight. Again, it was mid-morning when the first massive attack developed, three formations — 300 aircraft — crossing into Kent. There they parted, Dornier 17s of II/KG 2 heading for Hornchurch as Spitfires harried their escort. Other raiders attempted to reach the Thames Valley and East and South London. Many Hurricanes, and the Spitfires of 64 and 65 Squadrons, engaged them. Over Deal a furious engagement ensued between 266 Squadron's Spitfires and Messerschmitts of JG26. The Spitfire squadron was first caught at a grave disadvantage, five of its Spitfires being shot down including that of the leader, Squadron Leader Wilkinson, as the Messerschmitts bore down upon them.

Later that day extremely damaging dive-bomber raids were delivered on the aerodromes at Lee-on-Solent and Gosport causing much damage. Stukas were responsible for more at Tangmere, and Ju 88s escorted by Bf 110s were also operational in the area. In what had now become traditional style the Hurricanes went for the Stukas — destroying seven and damaging three — while Spitfires drove off their escort. Ventnor radar station was once more damaged, despite an attempt by Spitfires of 152 Squadron to prevent it, their defence being thwarted by the tough fighting of the Bf 109s. Then came yet another heavy engagement, Hurricane squadrons and the Spitfires of 64 Squadron routing Heinkel He 111s of KG 27 and their escorting Bf 110s over Sussex. More Spitfires, of 610 Squadron, drove off a Ju 88 trying to bomb Biggin Hill.

To round off the day's operations, in which the Luftwaffe flew 1,720 sorties — 400 by bombers — cannon-armed Spitfires of 19 Squadron shot down two Bf 110s off Harwich. By nightfall 47 enemy aircraft had certainly been destroyed in combat, for the loss of eleven Hurricanes and eleven Spitfires. Spitfires were responsible for the destruction of at least seventeen attackers, nine of them Bf 109s.

Intent now upon smashing Fighter Command, the largest concentration of enemy aircraft yet seen assembled over the Pas de Calais during the morning of 18 August. Soon after noon 54 Squadron's Spitfires headed off and were soon facing 300 raiders over Kent. Despite the odds, the Squadron did its best. At the same

Spitfire production 30 June 1940 to 26 October 1940
June 30-July 6 — *32*
Week ending July 13 — *30*, 20 — *41*, 27 — *37*
Week ending August 3 — *41*, 10 — *41*, 17 — *31*, 24 — *44*, 31 — *37*
Week ending September 7 — *36*, 14 — *38*, 21 — *40*, 28 — *34*
Week ending October 5 — *32*, 12 — *31*, 19 — *25*, 26 — *42*

time Hurricanes of 32 Squadron and 610's Spitfires attacked Do 17s making a low level assault upon Biggin Hill. Two enemy bombers were brought down and two crashed in the Channel. Another three of nine attacking Dorniers made forced landings in France. Meanwhile Ju 88s were busy cratering Biggin Hill as Flight Lieutenant Stanford Tuck in Spitfire *N3040* arrived. Quickly he turned upon the attackers, shooting down a Ju 88 before his aircraft was hit and he was forced to bale out. Kenley, too, had come under similar attack, and its Spitfires (of 64 Squadron) had to land between the bomb craters.

Come the afternoon of the 18th and once more the Solent and Portsmouth areas received attention, Ju 87s and '88s making for the Isle of Wight then splitting formations to bomb Ford, Gosport, Thorney Island and Poling radar station. Luckily Hurricanes arrived there just in time to interrupt the assault. As the German bombers reformed for their homeward run, Spitfires of 152 and 602 Squadrons as well as Hurricanes engaged them while 234 Spitfire Squadron tackled the fighter escort. Casualty lists showed that sixteen Ju 87s were destroyed and that two more crashed in France. Six Stukas were credited to 152 Squadron, three to No 602. The Messerschmitt escort had shot down four Spitfires and two Hurricanes, but eight Bf 109s came down. In the evening Hurricanes and Spitfires drove off an intended raid on Croydon, 54 Squadron's Spitfires this time destroying two Bf 110s. The day's activity cost five Spitfires and 37 Hurricanes, six of the latter wrecked on the ground at Kenley.

Then the weather turned bad, and for once low cloud and rain in August could be counted a blessing, for it provided a welcome break in the fighting. During the pause, however, many more Bf 109s were brought into north-east France as the Luftwaffe leadership realized that much stronger fighter cover was needed if their bombers were to achieve the destruction of the RAF. Fighters would be useful, too, for the mounting of more frequent 'feints' over the Channel in continued attempts to wear out Britain's fighter pilots.

Fatigue, high stress, lack of rest, bombing of their aerodromes, possible attacks on their homes, were indeed taking a considerable toll of pilots. Between 8 and 18 August Fighter Command lost 154 pilots killed, missing or seriously wounded, and only 63 replacements arrived. The effect of seeing many a dear friend die alongside in circumstances almost too horrific to envisaged was also having a profound effect.

But it was a short break and on 24 August the roar of the fight spilled into Essex. He 111s and Ju 88s bombed Hornchurch, home of the Spitfires while He 111s and Do 17s attacked North Weald. Help from 12 Group's more northerly-based squadrons was requested, but by the time they had formed into their acclaimed large formation, valuable time had been wasted. Breaking off to do their best, six Spitfires of No 19 Squadron raced to North Weald independently to fight a group of Bf 110s, but it was a luckless gesture which highlighted the premier Spitfire squadron's misfortune.

Since June, 19 Squadron had persevered with twin cannon Spitfires. Fitting the 20 mm Hispanos into the thin wing was difficult. They had to be mounted on their sides which caused problems when spent cartridges were ejected. Few

Battle of Britain Spitfire Squadrons: bases and strengths

09:00 hours on given dates
Figures illustrate squadron strength/additional unserviceable aircraft.

10 Group	1 July 1940	1 August 1940	1 September 1940
92 Squadron	—	Pembrey 12/4	Pembrey 12/4
152	—	Warmwell 10/5	Warmwell 12/4
234	—	Exeter 10/0	Middle Wallop 12/5
609	—	Middle Wallop 11/5	Middle Wallop 11/5
11 Group			
41 Squadron	—	Hornchurch 10/6	—
54	Rochford 12/3	—	Hornchurch 11/5
64	Kenley 10/4	Kenley 12/4	—
65	Hornchurch 10/7	Hornchurch 11/5	—
72	—	—	Croydon 15/3
74	Hornchurch 10/7	Hornchurch 12/3	—
92	Pembrey 11/6	—	—
222	—	—	Hornchurch 12/3
234	St Eval 9/6	—	—
266	—	Tangmere 13/5	—
602	—	—	Westhampnett 12/4
603	—	—	Hornchurch 13/3
609	Northolt 15/2	—	—
610	Gravesend 14/3	Biggin Hill 12/3	—
616	—	—	Kenley 12/4
12 Group			
19 Squadron	Fowlmere 8/5	Fowlmere 9/6	Fowlmere 11/4
66	Coltishall 12/4	Coltishall 12/4	Coltishall 10/6
74	—	—	Wittering 11/5
222	Kirton-in-Lindsey 12/4	Kirton 14/3	—
266	Wittering 8/5	—	Wittering 8/4
611	Digby 3/11	Digby/Ternhill 17	Digby 12/6
13 Group			
41 Squadron	Catterick 11/6	—	Catterick 14/3
54	—	Catterick 11/3	—
64	—	—	Leconfield 12/6
72	Usworth 12/4	Acklington 10/5	—
152	Acklington 8/4	—	—
602	Drem 12/4	Drem 11/4	—
603	Turnhouse 10/6	Turnhouse 11/4	—
610	—	Acklington 9/2	—
616	Church Fenton 11/4	Leconfield 12/4	—

rounds could be fired before the gun breeches jammed, and on this occasion only two Spitfires were able to fire. Nevertheless, three enemy fighters were claimed, and there was no doubt that when the guns did fire the results could be spectacular.

In battle the unexpected always had to be contemplated. Spitfires of 609 Squadron were engaging Bf 110s supporting raids over Dorset on 25 August, when the Ace of Spades Geschwader, JG 53, suddenly bounced them, damaging two Spitfires. But such was the manoeuvrability of the British fighters that they were able to turn quickly upon their Bf 109 attackers and damage a couple before resuming the former engagement, shooting down a Bf 110 and pouring damaging fire into another five. If the Luftwaffe wanted even more proof that the RAF was not a spent force it had only to return!

That it most assuredly did, for the numbers of attacking enemy aircraft were now greater than ever and when seven Spitfires hastily scrambled from Kenley on 26 August they almost immediately faced over fifty '109s. As the Squadron climbed into a favourable up-sun position, it was joined by another five Spitfires. But danger was nearer than any of the British pilots realized for suddenly thirty more 109s dived upon the Spitfires, destroying seven and killing two of their pilots. It was left to 54 and 610 Squadrons to even the score later, when near Ramsgate they picked off at least six Messerschmitt 109s.

If the RAF fighter force was to be put out of action — and without achieving that an invasion of England would be impossible — fighter stations north of London would have to be neutralized. Debden, Hornchurch and North Weald were raided on 26 August and then, early on 31 August Debden and Duxford became the targets. Anti-aircraft gunners did well, and drove the Dorniers away from Duxford. Soon after they had jettisoned their bombs and turned for home 19 Squadron's cannon Spitfires engaged the escorting Bf 110s. This time gun stoppages were so serious that return fire was able to bring down two Spitfires which were in position to fire and couldn't. Only one Messerschmitt was claimed. Later that day Spitfires of 54 Squadron were bombed as they scrambled from Hornchurch, and in a fight to protect Biggin Hill 222 Squadron lost two of its aircraft but destroyed a couple of Bf 109s.

That Spitfire losses were not higher is surprising for many an inexperienced young pilot, perhaps only in his late teens, or a pilot unaccustomed to fighters was posted into the front line in the hour of desperate need. His initiation to squadron life and the cruel fight were sometimes combined. Usually the Flight or Squadron Commander flew with him on a training combat sortie, for pilots from 7 Operational Training Unit often had incomplete training. He would be taught the rudimentary rules of combat and receive up to the minute advice from those in action daily. Sadly, all too often, new pilots would be picked off during their first fight. Survive, and one was on the way to life and success.

Each day repeated hoards of enemy aircraft made deeper penetrations. During the peak days of 30 and 31 August, around 1,600 enemy were counted, but never were there more than 400 bomber flights — showing how highly the Germans respected the British fighters which were far from wiped out. Between 24 August and 6 September there was only one day when less than 600 daylight sorties were flown against Britain. There was not the slightest let up in the fight, saturation attacks by waves of raiders causing our fighters to tackle the foe at odds of four or five to one. This was the most dangerous period of the battle for, with heavy loss of

RAF formations which trained Spitfire pilots

No 6 Operational Training Unit formed at Hawarden 15 June 1940 with three Flights each of six Spitfires and became 57 OTU (Day OTU, Spitfire) on 28 December 1940.

No 8 (Photo reconnaissance) Operational Training Unit formed 18 May 1942 at Fraserburgh from the PRU Conversion Flight, Squires Gate, and the PRU Advanced Training Flight, Detling. Moved to Dyce 9 to 11 February 1943. To Haverford West in January 1945, disbanded there 31 January 1947.

No 41 Operational Training Unit specialized in fighter-reconnaissance training and on 25 July 1944 was officially switched from a Mustang to a Spitfire unit. Based at Hawarden, Cheshire. To Chilbolton 23 March 1945, after a Day Fighter Wing (at half OTU strength) was hived off to open at Poulton on 1 February 1945. On 29 May, fighter-reconnaissance training was switched to 61 OTU. No 41 OTU closed 26 May 1945.

No 52 Operational Training Unit switched to a Spitfire establishment in November 1941. Based at Aston Down, where it closed on 10 August 1943. At the satellite station, Chedworth, the Fighter Leaders' School opened on 15 January 1943, and as the School of Tactics later moved to Aston Down.

No 53 Operational Training Unit opened as a Spitfire OTU in 81 Group at Heston on 11 March 1941. On 1 July 1941 it moved to Llandow and on 7 April 1942 its satellite station, Rhoose, opened. On 17 May 1943, 53 OTU moved to Kirton-in-Lindsey using Caistor and Hibaldstow as satellites. 53 OTU closed on 15 May 1945.

No 57 Operational Training Unit was formed from 7 OTU which entered No 81 Group on 28 December 1940 and became 57 OTU, a Day Fighter Unit at Hawarden. Moved to Eshott 10 November 1942. Satellite opened then at Boulmer. Training ceased 15 May 1945 and 57 OTU closed 6 June 1945.

No 58 Operational Training Unit opened at Grangemouth on 1 January 1941, and its satellite at Balado Bridge on 23 March 1942. It closed on 5 October 1943 and became No 2 Combat Training Wing, then No 2 Tactical Exercise Unit before closing on 25 June 1944. Balado Bridge closed 4 June 1944. No 58 OTU re-opened at Poulton on 12 March 1945 and closed on 20 July 1945, training having ceased on 22 May.

No 61 Operational Training Unit opened at Heston on 1 July 1941 and moved to Rednal on 15 April 1942 taking Mountford Bridge as its satellite station. It moved to Keevil on 16 June 1945, and formed the basis of the post-war 203 Advanced Flying School and later the fighter-reconnaissance element of 226 Operational Conversion Unit.

Wartime acclimatization training for Spitfire pilots in the Mediterranean Theatre was given at 71 OTU, 73 OTU and 74 OTU formed on 18 October 1941 as an off-shoot of 71 OTU.

life, airfields being seriously damaged at last and fighter output now being exceeded by losses, the advantage was swinging towards the enemy. Three more weeks of such sustained powerful effort would have exhausted British reserves and that would have brought disaster.

In the late afternoon of 1 September a small group of Dorniers delivered a vicious attack upon Biggin Hill, one 250 kg bomb bursting on a concrete ceiling and smashing the operations room. Next day Hornchurch was again raided and on the 3rd, North Weald was badly hit. No 19 Squadron tried in vain to use its two-cannon Spitfires to defend the station. When guns of only two out of eight Spitfires fired, the Squadron turned for home in despair, only to be cheered by the news that eight-gun Spitfires would be replacing them. In a strange twist to their history, some of these luckless cannon aeroplanes were re-engined, modified, and as Spitfire Vs, played a very important part in Fighter Command's 1941 war.

Illogically, the Luftwaffe had left alone the main fighter aircraft factories, but now, attention was directed against them, with a raid on the Hurricane works. German belief was that now that Fighter Command was all but smashed and its airfields were wrecked, a switch should be made to destroying fighter production. It was the start of a series of monumental blunders.

With the change in strategy came a noticeable alteration in enemy tactics, as a spate of small formations made widespread attacks — and still encountered our fighters. Messerschmitt 109s were sticking close to the vulnerable bombers, and even guarding the Bf 110 fighters which were no match for the British machines. The intensity of the fight, heavy losses and widespread exhaustion were as much evident in the Luftwaffe's ranks as in the British. That the invasion of Britain was imminent also was clear when, to bolster his own morale and that of High Command, Fieldmarshal Göring arrived in the Pas de Calais to witness the biggest formation of bombers so far launched setting off for England.

Bombastic, unpleasant and not all that bright, the utterly misguided commander had ordered a tremendous onslaught upon London. Believing, against all the evidence to which he must have had access, that Fighter Command was finished and that the fighter stations and interception control systems were beaten beyond repair, he had decided to order the attack to be switched against the British will to resist invasion.

In mid-afternoon of 7 September 348 German bombers escorted by 617 fighters set off in a twenty-mile-wide stream. After sweeping around the Foreland in impeccable formation the huge armada, stepped up from 14,000 to 23,000 ft, came in along the Thames towards the capital. Against this vast array Fighter Command, far from beaten, hurled 21 fighter squadrons. The best that could be done was to pick off enemy aircraft on the flanks, perhaps reduce the effectiveness of fighter cover then tackle the bombers as they flew homewards. In an attempt to prevent such a manoeuvre, escorting Bf 110s turned away. As the bombers battered London's East End, concentrating upon Woolwich, West Ham and London Docks, Bf 109s in profusion weaved around protectingly. That such

---

Spitfire battle casualties, summer 1940

First figure shows number of aircraft damaged and repairable, second figure shows aircraft lost in action or damaged beyond repair.

Week ending July 4 — *1/2*, 11 — *8/13*, 18 — *9/5*, 25 — *9/13*
Week ending August 1 — *8/14*, 8 —

8/15, 15 — *30/33*, 22 — *32/34*, 29 — *15/40*
Week ending September 5 — *45/66*, 12 — *28/32*, 19 — *20/22*, 26 — *21/20*
Week ending October 3 — *19/26*, 10 — *15/22*, 17 — *12/20*, 24 — *5/9*, 31 — *18/20*, Totals *353/406*

things really happened over Tower Bridge, that blazing sugar engulfed the streets, billions of slivers of glass rent the air, and that from hitherto unimaginable conflagrations sufficient smoke belched to turn a summer's day into night, it now seems almost impossible to believe.

Paradoxically, the response was not one of fear laced with desires for peace and retreat. Instead, the raid enormously strengthened the resolve of the nation that there must be no surrender, just total application to ensure ultimate victory. That common cry, 'Where are the fighters?', came now in the belief that whenever they appeared the enemy would have no hope of survival. And from this date, it seems, the Spitfire came to enshrine all our hopes. It looked good, it was good, and the enemy feared it as much as he envied it. In fact it was also to the numerically greater Hurricane that we owe our survival. Not for long, though, would the disparity in numbers remain, for the Spitfire was destined to overtake its mate.

By the end of that terrible day fourteen Spitfires and eighteen Hurricanes were no more, and 38 raiders had been shot down and almost as many more put out of action. Almost unnoticed, off the island of Walcheren, Spitfire IIs of 266 Squadron had destroyed a Do 215 nearly home after a photo reconnaissance flight. This was the first combat undertaken using the new type of Spitfire whose best performance came 4,000 ft higher than that of the Mk I. That development was very important now that battle was taking place at ever increasing altitudes. But upon trends there was little time to muse, for the vast fires in London clearly showed that the Luftwaffe was now fighting the British people, and not concentrating on fighter stations alone. The Luftwaffe, to its terrible cost, permitted Fighter Command to rest and recuperate before the planned invasion.

Playing a vitally important part in survival, fighter production in the week following the London raid exceeded fighter losses. On a typical Spitfire squadron there would normally have been 26 pilots; at this time there were usually only sixteen. To bolster strength, pilots were now being posted into front line squadrons from those in reserve. Narrow indeed was the margin now between collapse and survival.

Once committed to fighting the entire nation, there could be no turning back. In the new conditions ambitious 92 Squadron's Spitfires forsook distant Pembrey for Biggin Hill and such was the Squadron's ardour that in the next two weeks it lost nineteen Spitfires, saw five of its pilots killed and had five seriously wounded for the claim of sixteen enemy aircraft.

Inclement weather, and increased use of Do 17s and He 111s amongst the bomber force assembled for night raids upon London, resulted in daylight formation attacks increasingly involving only the faster Ju 88s, fighters and fighter-bombers. Although different in application, the German daylight onslaught was nevertheless intensively maintained and obviously heading towards the ultimate strike upon Britain. On 15 September, the climax came.

It was a beautiful day, with early fighter patrols seeking reconnoitring intruders. Quiet hours followed, but they were accompanied by a sense of deep foreboding. At mid-morning radar stations spotted the enemy gathering as around 100 Dorniers with huge fighter support headed for the Kent coast where

Spitfires known to have been in squadron hands on 15 September 1940

(Traditionally 'Battle of Britain Day')

19 Squadron: *N3039, N3238, N3265, P9386, P9431, R6991, X4059, X4070★ X4170, X4179, X4237, X4331, X4336, X4351, X4352*

41 Squadron: *K9890, N3059, N3123, N3266, P9324★, P9500, R6604, R6610, R6611, R6619, R6755, R6887, X4068, X4101, X4338, X4345, X4346*

54 Squadron: *L1042, N3176, P9506, P9558, P9559, R6709, R6814, R6893, R6895, R6898, R6899, R6973, R6981★, X4235, X4274, X4317, X4318, X4319*

64 Squadron: *L1073, P9450, P9557, P9564, R6639, R6683, R6700, R6792, R6975, X4032*

65 Squadron: *K9789, K9904, N3161, N3163, P9454, P9562, R6712, R6714, R6775, R6803, R6883, R6886, R6978, R6982, X4015, X4232*

66 Squadron: *N3035, N3121, R6602, R6716, R6771, R6779, R6800, R6925, R6927, X4020, X4176, X4255, X4266, X4320, X4321, X4322, X4326, X4339, X4419*

72 Squadron: *K9847, K9929, K9940, K9989, N3068, N3094, N3229, P9338, P9457, P9460, R6704, R6710, R6777, R6881, R6984, X4063, X4337, X4340, X4413, X4416*

74 Squadron: *P7306, P7310, P7312, P7316, P7329, P7352, P7355, P7356, P7360, P7361, P7362, P7363, P7364, P7366, P7367, P7368, P7370, P7373, R6606, R6840, X4027, X4167*

92 Squadron: *K9951, K9953, L1014, N3193, N3248, N3283, P9513, P9544, R6616, R6622★, R6760, R6767, X4037, X4038, X4039, X4069*

★ Spitfires written off during the day.

152 Squadron: *K9881, K9882, K9900, K9982, L1072, P9427, R6764, R6907, R7016, X4017, X4169, X4171, X4246, X4247, X4355*

222 Squadron: *K9878, K9939, K9993, L1031, L1089, N3119, N3164, N3203, N3233, P9447, P9469, P9492, P9542, R6638, R6685, R6772, R6773, X4024, X4058, X4265, X4331*

234 Squadron: *N3057, N3191, N3276, P9508, P9519, R6896, R6959, R7017, X4036, X4243, X4244, X4251, X4387*

266 Squadron: *L1011, N3118, N3245;* Mk IIs : *P7286, P7288, P7294, P7295, P7297, P7309, P7311, P7313, P7324, P7325, P7327, P7328, P7350, P7365*

602 Squadron: *K9833, L1002, L1040, N3228, N3242, P9423, P9446, P9515, R6780, R6839, X4104, X4160, X4269, X4382, X4390, X4412*

603 Squadron: *K9803, K9963, L1076, N3267, P9553, R6626, R6836, R7019★, X4250, X4259, X4323, X4324★, X4347, X4348, X4349, X4415*

609 Squadron: *K9997, L1048, L1065, L1096, N3221, N3223, R6631, R6690, R6699, R6915, R6961, R6979, X4106, X4165*

610 Squadron: *K9947, K9970, K9975, L1009, L1037, N3124, P9451, R6599, R6806, R6891, R6976, R6993, X4011, X4065, X4067, X4105, X4238*

611 Squadron: Mk II: *P7281, P7282, P7283, P7284, P7285, P7291, P7300, P7301, P7302, P7303, P7305, P7314, P7321, P7322, P7323, P7354, P7371, P7374, P7376*

616 Squadron: *K9996, L1001, L1034, L1036, N3058, N3066, R6686, R6778, R6963, R6980, X4056, X4172, X4174, X4186, X4328, X4329, X4330, X4388*

Top X4330:G *lands in company with another 92 Squadron Spitfire during the Battle of Britain* (IWM).

Above *Spitfire R6800, 'LZ:N', (which served with 66 Squadron from 26 July 1940 until shot down near Westerham, Kent on 17 October 1940) watches a companion landing at Gravesend in October 1940* (RAF Museum P017391).

Spitfires challenged them. Called in to help 11 Group, 12 Group's Wing included two Spitfire squadrons and these burst through the fighter screen protecting the flanks to force apart the bomber formation. In chaos the enemy bombed then fled for home, engagements ensuing over a wide area. Individual combats soon produced for friend and foe the very type of risky engagement about which all were warned.

Back came more raiders during the afternoon, famed Adolf Galland's JG 26 and JG 54, 'The Green Hearts' escorting about 150 Dorniers and Heinkels, again bound for London. Despite their losses of the morning, British fighters responded in strength, 11 Group's 170 Hurricanes and Spitfires pestering the enemy but this time failing to split his ranks. Then, with the sky over East London a mass of vapour trails, Spitfires and Hurricanes of the Duxford Wing swooped. They were soon joined by eight more squadrons which attacked head-on. That sort of assault the bomber formation could not endure for long and it turned, leaving its fighter escort embroiled in the fiercest combat possible, rapidly depleting its limited fuel and forcing the '109s to break off the battle in despair. Too late to achieve much, German fighter reserves arrived. The victorious Fighter Command was exhausted.

The sight of over 300 RAF fighters when German official claims were that Fighter Command had been smashed, must have been a bitter blow to the Luftwaffe crews. Clearly, their losses, the sight of comrades dying or brutally wounded, and of enormous courage expended to little purpose was as bad for them as for the RAF.

A second afternoon attack involved a smaller bomber force which attempted to bomb Portland. Warmwell's Spitfires battled with He 111s, while a group of Bf 110 fighter-bombers of the specialized *Erpro* 210 tried without success to destroy the Woolston Spitfire works.

As evening wore on the sky over East Anglia was covered by high cloud; in reality it was being doused by hundreds of decaying and merging contrails. I had spent that day at Bedford, and as we motored home, and dusk closed in, the sky to the south began reflecting the glow of London burning. Already the wireless had proclaimed a great victory. Then, late that night came stupendous news: 185 enemy aircraft had been destroyed during the day. It was indeed time for elation. Standing in our garden I could hear cries of joy from neighbours at the news of such a tremendous RAF victory. But at what cost one could but guess for the sky south was ever a brighter orange.

In fact about 54 enemy aircraft had been destroyed, 21 of them Bf 109s and many more damaged. During the chaotic fight it was easy for more than one pilot to claim the same enemy aircraft, and confusion could easily arise. Verification could only be ascertained after the capture of Luftwaffe documents and even then it was, for each day of the battle, a lengthy, painstaking task that was never to reveal the exact truth. But that the victory had been enormous there was no doubt. It cost but six Spitfires and nineteen Hurricanes. Most important of all, this great victory discouraged the notion that German forces could now seize the British Isles. Four days later the invasion was 'postponed'.

The Battle of Britain was far from over, but the daylight battle had now undoubtedly been won. Vicious bombing and fighting was to follow, including the immensely damaging attacks upon the Supermarine factories at Southampton. But gradually the contest developed into high level dogfights particularly between Spitfires and Bf 109s. When in October 1940 the fighting reached 30,000 ft or more only the Spitfire could really cope — just. Something would have to be done about that, and fast. Only better Spitfires would be of any value.

Spitfire Mk II (1,150 hp Merlin XII) — salient details

Wing span 36 ft 10 in. Length 29 ft 11 in. Height (max) 11 ft 5½ in. Wing aerofoil section NACA 2200. Tailplane span 10 ft 6 in, area 31.46 sq ft. Wing area 242 sq ft, dihedral 6°. Wheel track 5 ft 8½ in. Engine coolant: 70% distilled water, 30% ethylene glycol. Suitable propellers: Rotol RX5/1CS 10 ft 3 in diameter, magnesium alloy, or RX5/3 CS 10 ft 3 in diameter, wood (Jablo type), or DH 5/39A CS of 10 ft 9 in diameter (Dural).

Chapter 7
Making the Spitfire unbeatable

More height, more speed, more range and a heavier punch. All of these the Spitfire would need, to continue as a top fighter. Whereas the slight improvement shown by the Spitfire II was not nearly enough, the Spitfire III with its faster climb and ability to fly higher and two-speed blower Merlin XX sounded good. Its clipped wings enabled it to roll faster, but when the idea of also fitting four cannon was introduced, fears arose that the existing Spitfire airframe, safe to about 7,200 lb, would no longer be strong enough. But in the closing weeks of 1940 day fighting proved certain need for a new Spitfire, and 1,000 Mk IIIs were ordered. That order was more of an indication that a new version was needed than an intent, for Merlin XXs were already earmarked to improve other aircraft, in particular the Hurricane.

Luckily there were other new Merlins in the offing, in particular the 40 and 60 series. By fitting a special blower on the Merlin X Rolls-Royce produced the highly reliable 1,470 hp Merlin 45 giving its best performance in the 20,000 ft range and this engine the existing Spitfire airframe could accommodate. That such a combination was likely to be successful seemed certain and, just before Christmas 1940, mass production of the latest version of the Spitfire was ordered. Proof of the excellence of the idea was given when a Mk 1, powered by the new engine, was test flown. It turned out to be nearly 20 mph faster and to have a ceiling 2,000 ft higher. By April 1941 the Merlin 45 Spitfire was to be in

---

The Spitfire II

Originally the designation of the first Griffon Spitfire, the Mk II instead had a Merlin XII (1,150 hp at 14,500 ft) driving a Rotol CS propeller. This combination gave the Spitfire an additional 2,000 ft ceiling. The Spitfire II was to be the first powered by a Merlin variant running on 100 octane petrol and fitted with a Coffman cartridge starter. (Merlin IIs and IIIs ran on 85 octane fuel.) Main 'prototype' K9791.

All Castle Bromwich built. P7280, first example, initially flown in May 1940, sent to Boscombe Down 27 June 1940. P7286, first example delivered to a squadron, went to 152 Squadron on 17 July 1940. First to be fully equipped — 611 Squadron in late August 1940, 266 Squadron early September, then 74 Squadron. First operational deployment — 31 August by 611 Squadron at Duxford. 354 aircraft delivered by end of 1940.

Above *Spitfire IIa 'YT:L', P7665 of 65 Squadron. This aircraft failed to return from a fighter sweep over France on 5 February 1941 (IWM).*

Right *A standard, late production Spitfire 1, R7155 'Kikuyu-Emlu' built in January 1941 (IWM).*

Below *Spitfire IIa P8479, one of the many presentation aircraft. This machine was paid for by British Glues & Chemicals whose badge it bears. After serving with 74 Squadron it was used by 61 OTU, and, briefly, 277 ASR Squadron.*

production, to face the expected Luftwaffe spring offensive. Fighter Command was convinced that the new type would outfly any Messerschmitt 109.

Much improvement of the Spitfire also resulted from inspired yet painstaking work. Banking and turning the aircraft at high speed, for example, had not been easy and required quite strong force on the control stick. Any speed increase would make this problem worse, and especially in a fast dive during combat. Lots of small changes were tried, but the breakthrough came when metal-covered ailerons were tested. As many Spitfires as possible were ordered to have them as fast as they could be fitted. So, at the end of 1940, the immediate future looked good.

To get the new Spitfire into use quickly, another bright idea was put forward. Those 23 'useless' two-cannon Spitfire Is which 19 Squadron used during the Battle of Britain and now languishing in storage units, could be re-engined with Merlin RM5s (Mk 45s to the RAF) which gave 1,205 bhp at 15,500 ft. At the same time intensive work would be undertaken to make their guns a going concern. By adding a bulge on the top surface of the wing, the drum containing the 20 mm shells for the Hispano cannon could just be accommodated allowing the gun to sit more sensibly and the problem of used cartridges jamming in the breech avoided. Operating weight of the new cannon Spitfire, which in February 1941 was named the Mk V, was 6,460 lb. It was lighter than the Mk III even when four .303 in Browning guns were added along the wings.

Test flying of another Spitfire fitted with a Merlin 45 showed its top speed to be 369 mph at 25,000 ft, a height it could reach in 8 1/2 minutes. In just under a quarter of an hour it climbed to 35,000 ft. First to have the Mk V was No 92 Squadron which had so quickly distinguished itself in the later stages of the Battle of Britain and was based at Biggin Hill. Production Mk Vs began to reach squadrons in May 1941.

The rate of cannon building, however, was slow and great was the demand for them. Therefore Merlin 45 Spitfires leaving the production lines in February and March, other than the modified Mk Is and a handful of two cannon/four machine gun Mk Vbs delivered in March, had eight machine-guns, and were called Mk Vas. They carried more rounds of ammunition than the cannon Spitfires, giving, claimed some pilots, a greater chance of a wounding strike. In particular the famed Douglas Bader much preferred the Mk Va.

Spitfire Mk V — salient details

(F Mk V: Merlin 45, 46, 50 or 50A; LF Mk V Merlin 45, 50M or 55M) Wing span 36 ft 10 in (32 ft 2 in when clipped). Length 29 ft 11 in. Height to propeller tip 11 ft 5½ in. Track 5 ft 8½ in. Tailplane span 10 ft 6 in. Wing aerofoil section NACA 2200. Wing dihedral 6°. Gross fin area 4.61 sq ft. Gross rudder area 8.23 sq ft. Suitable propeller types — DK CS 5/39 or Rotol RX 5/10. Fuselage fuel tanks — upper 48 gallons, lower 37 gallons. Auxiliary drop tanks — carry either 30 or 90 gallons in slipper tanks, or 17 gallon ferrying tank and 29 gallons in rear fuselage. Mk Va and Vb — different mainplanes and gun layouts; Mk Vc had universal gun layout mainplane.

A particularly important task for Spitfires was protection of coastal shipping and arriving convoys. 130 Squadron's Mk Vbs can be seen here at bleak Perranporth in Cornwall (RAF Museum P015717).

The wing intended for the Spitfire III could contain either machine-guns, cannon or a mixture of the two. Known as the 'Universal Wing' it was far superior to the earlier types because instead of eight Brownings it could carry four Brownings and two belt-fed cannon or four cannon. By carefully arranging the cannon and placing tubes onto their barrels, they could be staggered in position in the wings. Take away all machine-guns and it was possible to fit two cannon in each mainplane. There was, however, a problem in heating the guns in the four-cannon layout and most of those Spitfires, Mk Vcs, were used overseas in hot areas. Performance was also reduced by the weight of the guns, the fully armed Mk Vc fitted for service in tropical conditions having a top speed of 347 mph at 18,000 ft.

If the only major change needed to produce the Mk V concerned its engine, the question arose — could the Mk II, of which 921 were completed, at least have the new gun layouts? The answer was 'yes' — if enough wings and guns could be built. Accordingly, a hundred sets of the drum-fed, two-cannon four-machine-gun wings were ordered in February 1941 for the Spitfire IIs. By July 1941 at least 258 cannon-armed Spitfire IIbs had been produced.

The Mk V was a clever innovation, but what if the air battles of 1941 regularly took place at over 30,000 ft, even above 40,000 ft? At such heights pilots would need pressurized suits to avoid the same 'bends' that affect divers. Extra effort would be needed to cope, and their efficiency would fall. They would feel very uncomfortable even in suits, which, after each flight, would take a long time to dry out. Fit a pressure suit and there was the problem of a pilot having to be supplied

Eyes in the skies — the photo-reconnaissance Spitfires

The earliest of these carried cameras beneath their wings, and a few saw service in France before the British withdrawal in 1940. By then camera fits in Spitfire fuselages were being tried, at Farnborough and the Photographic Development Unit, Heston. Each aircraft here was an individual, each was based on the Spitfire Mk 1 and identified by letter and not mark number. When a standard design was achieved the designation Mk IV was applied to the photographic reconnaissance variant based upon the Mk V. Some Mk Vs were also modified for the task and called PR VIIs. When the Merlin 61 Spitfire was introduced a PR version powered by the 60-series engine was devised, known as the Mk XI. A few Mk IXs were also fitted with cameras, and some specialized older airframes were designated PR Mk XIII. The Griffon PR aircraft was the very long range sophisticated PR Mk XIX.

Above *The Spitfire PR-X, developed from the Mk VII, and of which sixteen were produced, had a pressure cabin.*

Below EN654, *a PR Mk XI, served with 16 Squadron from October 1943 to September 1944, securing photographs with particular significance for the invasion of France and in connection with the campaign against V-1 sites* (RAF Museum 5983-3).

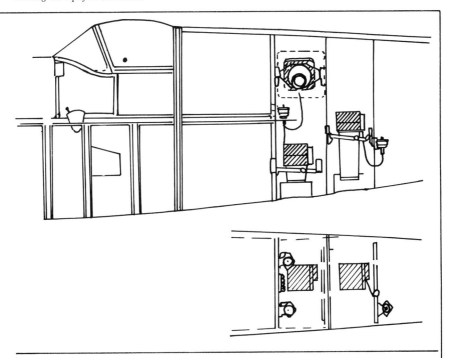

Above *Early PR Spitfires had individual-
istic camera installations but by the middle of
the war standard layouts were usually to be
found. Most photo-reconnaissance Spitfires
carried their cameras in the rear fuselage.
Illustrated is the 'G' Type camera installation, showing the arrangement of three F.24
cameras, two set central and vertical and one
on the fuselage port side for shooting obliques.
Cameras were fitted between fuselage frames
Nos 13 and 15. Electric motors to operate
shutter blinds, and their leads, can be seen,
and the (usually) Type 25 mountings. The
pilot sighted his oblique camera using a
circular mark on the cockpit canopy.*

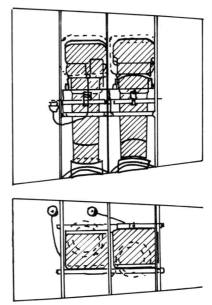

Right *Illustrated is the twin F.52 camera
installation which Spitfire PR XIs could
carry, the cameras with 36 in lenses being
slightly tilted for maximum area coverage
whilst retaining some overlap.*

Spitfire over Berlin

Surprising as it may seem, the first Allied aircraft to reach Berlin in daylight was a Spitfire of the little-known No 3 Photographic Reconnaissance Unit. Formed at Oakington on 16 November 1940, 3 PRU was part of Bomber Command — unlike No 1 PRU and later its hived-off Benson-based squadrons which were part of Coastal Command. The tasks for 3 PRU were damage assessment flights after bomber raids, photo-reconnaissance for Bomber Command and night reconnaissance which it was to develop.

Strength of 3 PRU included six Spitfires, initially Mk IIs fitted with one or two 7 x 7 in cameras and a 20 in focal length fuselage-carried camera. Unarmed, like nearly all PR Spitfires, they carried additional fuel tanks, extra oil and more oxygen to enable long duration sorties. According to the modifications, PRU Spitfires were designated Type A to G and also known as PR Mk 1 and VII respectively. The early PR Spitfires were either 'one-offs' or built in small batches initially for the Photographic Development Unit at Heston, or No 1 PRU Benson. Some were later to have Merlin 45s and 46s and eventually it was the PR Mk IV which became the normal Merlin 45/46 PR Spitfire.

3 PRU received its first example, Spitfire 'C' X4385, on 23 November 1940. It had an F8 20 in lens camera installed in the fuselage, two 8 in lens F24s in the starboard wing, and had two extra thirty-gallon fuel tanks. More Type 'C' Spitfires

followed, then on 9 January 1941 came the first Type 'F', X4712, with an F8 (ie Film Camera, Type 8) in the rear fuselage and a thirty-gallon fuel tank in the starboard wing instead of F24 cameras. It carried five bottles of oxygen, and had an endurance of 4¾ hours.

3 PRU's first operational sortie, to Aachen on 29 November 1940, was flown by X4385 and its first loss (of X4386) came on 12 January 1941 when the aircraft failed to return from Bremen. A sudden thaw after winter snow and ice overtook Oakington on 22 January 1941 turning its surface into a quagmire. No 3 PRU then operated from Alconbury from where, on 14 March 1941, X4712 set off for the historic flight to Berlin. It flew first to Horsham St Faith where twenty gallons of fuel were taken aboard before the flight was resumed at 10:20. Berlin was reached at 12:25 and there, despite the mist, 95 shots were taken of the city.

At 14:40 Squadron Leader P.B.B. Ogilvie landed at Alconbury — with twenty gallons of fuel left. This historic Spitfire failed to return from a reconnaissance flight to Bremerhaven on 8 April. The unit, too, had a brief life, for in July 1941 it was absorbed by No 1 PRU, Benson to which it took its two remaining Spitfires Type 'C' (X4393 and X4493) with fuselage and wing cameras and its four Type 'F' Spitfires, X4494 (the first received with a Merlin 45), X4385, X4498 and X6902.

with oxygen as he made his way to the aircraft. No, that was no answer and in late January 1941 it was decided to install special pressurized cabins into some Spitfire Vs.

By April 1941 suggested additional modifications included a six-cannon wing with extended tips, resulting in a Spitfire weighing between 8,000 and 9,000 lb. A Mk V was taken off the production line, and at a cost of £2,000 fitted with a slightly pressurized cabin and a four-bladed propeller to use all the air available at very high levels. Most important, it had a special version of the Merlin RM5, the

Top *Spitfire Vb AB320, bearing prototype marking, served for trials with both the Vokes type tropical filter beneath its engine and long-range slipper tank.*

Above *Ready to go, a Spitfire Vb of 350 Squadron.*

Mk 46. Three days after the first flight on 4 July 1941 the prototype reached 38,000 ft. In September 1941 an initial fifty examples designated Mk VI were ordered, to be powered by the production type engine, the Merlin 47, but because of the weight problem none could have the Universal Wing, let alone six cannon. All would have the 'B' gun layout consisting of two cannon and four machine-guns.

At this time Rolls-Royce had another more powerful superb Merlin making excellent progress. In mid-1940, to give better performance at considerable

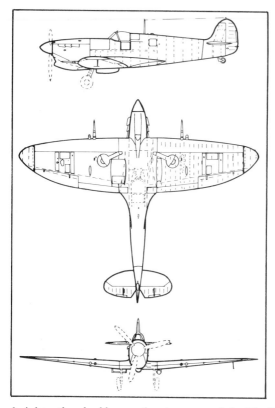

Left *The mid-war strengthened four-cannon Supermarine 349 Spitfire Vc, with tropical filter. The undercarriage is raked slightly more forward when extended, and the inner of the two Browning guns in each mainplane are sited slightly more outboard. Body length depended upon spinner type, the illustrated variant being 30 ft overall.*

Above right *Designed in April 1942, the 'pointed' wing was intended for high-flying Spitfires and fitted to Mks VI, VII, some VIIIs, a few Mk IXs and Griffon-engined prototypes.*

heights, they had begun development of the Merlin 60 series, a two-speed engine with a second supercharger. The purpose of the supercharger (or blower) was to maintain a certain pressure of petrol/air mixture in the engine, preventing loss of power as the engine flew higher. A two-speed supercharger thus offered high take-off power, and then a further range of maximum power at high altitudes. By increasing the pressure in the engine's induction system extra power could be obtained for a limited time. This was known as boost pressure, measured in lb/sq in.

June 1941 brought a major review of Spitfire development. With the Merlin 61 engine flying, the decision was taken to try this in a Spitfire Vb to improve its performance at over 25,000 ft. Fitting the engine lengthened the aircraft by nine inches, while the necessary intercooler between the cylinders and supercharger meant that another radiator to cool its water was required. The main radiator was under the starboard wing and now a second radiator was fitted beneath the port wing, housed alongside the oil cooler. This at last gave the Spitfire a symmetrical appearance. Due to the additional weight of the Merlin 61 the revised aircraft so powered was reckoned to need the strengthened airframe developed for the four-cannon Spitfire Vc.

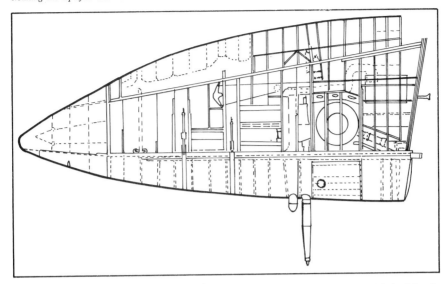

Very quickly, a new range of Spitfires had come about: the Mk VI high altitude fighter (Merlin 47); the Mk VII, Merlin 61 version of the Mk VI; the Mk VIII, a Merlin 61 version of the Mk Vc using the stronger B-type airframe; and the Mk IX, the adaptation of the Mk V powered by the Merlin 61 series. Rather surprisingly in view of the early success and attractiveness of the latter idea, it was not until late that year that official approval was given to powering the Mk Vb with a Merlin 61. Concern over the airframe's strength caused concern before events proved that belief unfounded.

A Merlin 61 was first flown in the ageing Spitfire Mk III prototype on 20 September 1941 and the results were astonishing. It readily took the aircraft to 42,500 ft, and calculations showed that the Mk IX would be 70 mph faster than the average Mk V and be able to fight at well over 10,000 ft higher. The news could not have come at a better time, for Spitfire pilots, flying operations over France intended to lure German fighters into battle and tie them down from fighting on the Russian front, were meeting a fast, new, German air-cooled radial-engined fighter, the Focke-Wulf Fw 190 which was 30 mph faster than the Spitfire V. Indeed, the only advantage Spitfire Vs possessed in combat with this adversary was their tighter turning circle; otherwise they were outclassed — for the present.

Publicly, leaks about the quality of the new opponent were derisively dismissed. The Luftwaffe, short of fighters, was said to be using aged Curtiss Hawk 75s taken

Spitfire VII — special points

F.Mk VII — Merlin 64; HF Mk VII — Merlin 71. Wing span 40 ft 2 in. Length 31 ft. 97 gallon fuel load in forward tanks, 28 gallons in wing tanks. 'C' armament wing, modified control surfaces. First production Spitfire to have retractable tailwheel.

Spitfire VIII and IX (early examples) compared

	Mk VIII	**Mk IX**
Length overall	30 ft 4½ in	31 ft 0½ in
Height	11 ft 8 in	11 ft 8 in
Wing span	36 ft 10 in	36 ft 10 in
All up weight	7,700 lb	7,238 lb
Wings	Strengthened, as for Mk Vc	Universal, as for Mk V
Tailwheel	retractable	fixed
Fuel normal	115 gal	85 gal
Drop tank fit	all examples	all except first six aircraft
Exhaust flame dampers	on all	not on first 100
Economical cruise range	525 miles	340 miles
Economical cruise range (+ 30 gal tank)	740 miles	550 miles

Standard Spitfire Mk IX — salient data and typical performance

Wing span 36 ft 10 in. Length 31 ft 0 ½ in. Height 11 ft 8 in. Wing area 242 sq ft. Weight empty 5,800 lb, weight loaded 7,500 lb. Top speed 408 mph at 25,000 ft. Initial climb 3,950 fpm. Service ceiling 43,000 ft. Fuel — 85 gallons in forward tanks; late 1944 75 gallon rear fuselage tank was optional.

Prototype Mk IX was *N3297* (ex Mk III) sent to Rolls-Royce on 29 July 1941 for conversion. Second prototype first flew 6 January 1942, subsequently two more Mk Vcs delivered for conversion.

The Spitfire VI

Development aircraft: **1** *N3053* Fitted with a Merlin 46 and four-bladed propeller. **2** *X4922* First flew 4 July 1941 — a Spitfire V with pressure cabin, Merlin 46, four-bladed propeller but no guns. Weight loaded 5,970 lb. Reached 39,900 ft in 27 minutes. Cockpit air pressure at 10,000 ft equivalent to that at 4,000 ft. Engine surge problems in August 1941 cured by fitment of pressurized fuel tanks. Pressure leak from cabin traced as coming from electric wiring core. **3** *R7120* Powered by a 1,415 hp Merlin 47 — a Mk 46 with improved blower and crankcase for pressure cabin equipment. RAE Farnborough aircraft for pressure cabin research, first flown November 1941.

Spitfire Mk VI (Merlin 47) salient data

Span 40 ft 2 in : Length overall 30 ft 2 in. Height to prop tip 11 ft 5 ½ in. Height to centre of prop boss 6 ft 1 in. Wing aerofoil NACA 2200, dihedral 6°. Tailplane span 10 ft 6 in, chord 4 ft. Fuselage maximum width 3 ft 5.8 in. Wing area including ailerons and flaps 248.5 sq ft. Flap area 15.6 sq ft. Undercarriage track 5 ft 8½ in. Propeller, Rotol four-blade CS Type R2/4F5/1 Jablo form, or R2/4F5/2 Dural, pitch range 35, diameter 10 ft 9 in. Fuel tanks, upper — 38 gallons, lower — 37 gallons. Oil — 5.8 gallons. All-up weight 6,738 lb. All had 'B' armament. Maximum speed 381 mph at 23,500 ft. Service release: April 1942 Original intention — production of 350 examples.

BR579, *a Spitfire HF VI of 124 Squadron* (IWM).

from the French in 1940. But the truth was too well known — here was something far superior to anything the RAF was using. How desperate now was the need for just such a fighter as the Merlin 61 Spitfire. That it must remain some way off was, however, clear when it was noticed that at heights between 17,000 and 25,000 ft, before the second supercharging power came in, performance was falling away. Luckily that could be cured by brief additional boost pressure when needed. So good did the Mk Vb/Merlin 61 combination prove to be that the RAF soon wanted to cancel all other Spitfire versions, but with only eight Merlin 61s available before March 1942 that was impossible.

The first production Mk VI emerged at the start of 1942, refinements brought by the Merlin 47 and four-bladed propeller enabling it to climb to 2,000 ft higher than its predecessors. The pressure cabin did little more than give the pilot the sensation of flying six miles high when he was eight miles up, so the ride was still far from comfortable. Four cannon would have made the Mk VI impossibly heavy, for its weight was already increased by the longer, pointed tip wings and pressure cabin. Indeed, additional strengthening was required before the Mk VI could come into service.

The sealed cockpit became stiflingly hot as the aircraft climbed, and necessary improvements witheld the aircraft's operational debut until mid-summer. Eventually only 124 and 616 Squadrons were fully equipped with Mk VIs, their prime role being to prevent high flying bombers from attacking Britain. Later, both squadrons along with No 131 received Merlin 60 or 70 series Spitfire VIIs. These had pressure cabins, pointed wing tips and broad chord pointed rudders. The high flying version (Merlin 71), with a top speed of 416 mph despite its weight of 7,875 lb loaded at take-off, could easily outfight a Fw 190. Some released Mk VIs were used to prevent high flying enemy aircraft observing naval movements around Scapa Flow.

Far more important than the Mk VIs and VIIs though was the Spitfire V fitted with a Merlin 61 and designated Mk IX. It was to 64 Squadron at Hornchurch

---

Spitfire VIII — salient data and typical performance

LF Mk VIII — Merlin 66; F Mk VIII — Merlin 61 (1,565 hp at 12,250 ft and 1,390 hp at 23,500 ft); HF Mk VIII — Merlin 70. Wing span 36 ft 10 in (few 40 ft 2 in). Length 30 ft 4 $\frac{1}{2}$ in. Height 11 ft 8 in. Wing area 242 sq ft. 'C' armament normal. 124 gallons internal fuel, including wing tankage. Top speeds: 391 mph at 15,000 ft, and, with full supercharger working, 414 mph at 27,200 ft. Speed at 40,000 ft, 354 mph (height reached after 34 minutes). Operational ceiling 38,100 ft, estimated absolute — 42,800 ft.

Had a compact tropical filter in place of large, bulky Vokes type of earlier Spitfires. All Supermarine built, almost all with broad chord-pointed rudder. Delivery began April 1943, first examples to 92 Squadron (HF VIIIs) and 145 Squadron (LF VIIIs) Mediterranean Theatre. Deliveries to Far East began in 1944 to replace Mk Vc.

---

that the first Spitfire IXbs were delivered in June 1942. Both choices were good and from that RAF station, object of much Battle of Britain bombing, the new Spitfires began offensive operations on 28 July. Two days later when covering Hurribombers the new Spitfires distinguished themselves by shooting down four Fw 190s over France. The Spitfire IX came into service just as the Americans commenced B-17 bombing raids on Occupied Europe and for many months the new-type Spitfires gave them fighter cover. As good as the Mk IX quickly proved to be, the RAF still wanted its refined version the Mk VIII — and by the end of 1942.

The Fw 190 performed best between 14,000 ft and 20,000 ft at which heights the Spitfire IX was not at its best. Improvement came when adjustments reduced the height at which the Merlin 60 series performed best, and many Spitfires were to be fitted with the resulting Merlin 66, an engine which functioned best between 10,000 and 20,000 ft. Although initially a high altitude engine, the power output of the 60 series was now being produced at lower levels and gave birth to a family of Spitfire IXs. The standard HF (High Flying) Mk IX had either a Merlin 61 or 63 while the (Low Flying) LF IX had a Merlin 66. For specialized high altitude fighting the HF IX became available powered by a Merlin 70 series engine. Of the three, the low altitude variant probably became the most useful fighter and ground attack aircraft and found itself in great demand to support the planned Allied advance into mainland Europe. In June 1943 Spitfire orders were changed to take account of this to the extent that three-quarters of the Spitfire VIIIs and IXs were to be engined with the Merlin 66.

In America production of the Rolls-Royce Merlin was undertaken on a massive scale by Packard Motors, primarily for use in the P-51 Mustang. Spitfire IXs with Packard Merlin 66s (known as Mk 266) and used for low and medium level operations were designated Mk XVI. The American engines were very similar to the British, apart from supercharger and some other relatively small changes. This meant that the engines were interchangeable, and remains useful for present-day Spitfire owners. Delivery of the Spitfire XVI began in October 1944, the aircraft entering service the following month with the Coltishall Wing which immediately used it for fighter-bomber strikes particularly against V-2 sites in the

Right *JF294, an early production Spitfire VIII, has pointed wing tips and overall blue high-altitude finish* (IWM).

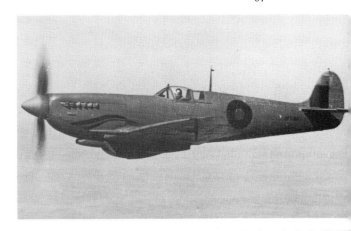

Below *Preparing a 74 Squadron Spitfire IXe for a sortie from a Belgian airfield early in 1945* (RAF Museum 6034–13).

Bottom *Spitfire IXs of 401 (RCAF) Squadron wallow in Continental mud, possibly at Heesch, in early 1945. For an aircraft not reckoned to be all that rugged, these seem to be surviving well!* (RAF Museum 6035–2).

Netherlands. All of this version were known as LF XVI, some featuring 'C' type armament and many type 'E'. Production continued until August 1945 which resulted in a large surplus of Mk XVIs for post-war use.

Extending the Spitfire's range

The Spitfire Mk 1 carried 85 gallons of fuel in two forward fuselage tanks, affording duration of about 1 ½ hours. First attempts to increase that involved fitting a small teardrop-shaped drop tank on each wing leading edge. Next came the Spitfire IIa(LR) with a large 30 gallon tank asymetrically fitted to its port wing. Such Spitfires served in 10 Group for lengthy patrols during operations off the south-west coast.

The first standard drop tank was the 30 gallon rectangular slipper tank which nestled under the wing centre section. This was largely superseded by the 45 gallon drop tank. To enable squadrons to operate Spitfires from Malta, they were taken to the Mediterranean and flown off aircraft carriers sailing off the Algerian coast. Entailing a journey of about 700 miles, 385 Spitfires (mainly Vcs for Nos 126, 185 and 249 Squadrons) set off between March and October 1942, and, aided by 90 gallon tanks, 367 arrived safely. Additionally, a few Spitfire Vs were fitted with a giant 170 gallon tank to enable them to make the 1,100 mile journey from Gibraltar to Malta in October 1942.

A variety of drop tanks was produced for Spitfires. 'A' depicts the 90-gallon tinned steel slipper drop tank (7 ft 2 in long, 3 ft wide) and 'B' the 60-gallon torpedo tank 9 ft 4½ in long and with a diameter of 18 in. Development, fitting and successful dropping of these tanks was quite a complicated business. Fuel lines and pump feed systems were of course needed.

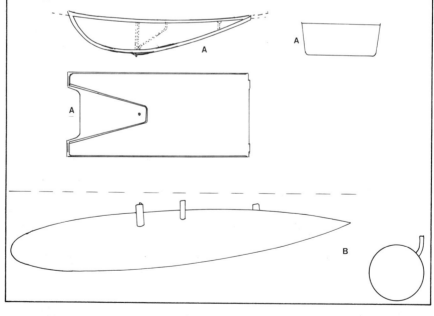

Above *The superb Mk 14, RM689, preserved in flying condition by Rolls-Royce, pursued by the Shuttleworth Collection's Mk Vc,* AR501.

Below *Another view of one of the Battle of Britain Flight's Mk 19s, PM631.*

Atmospheric shot of one of the Mk IXs used during the making of The Battle of Britain *film* (Spitfire Productions Ltd).

Left *Superb aerial shot of a late war Mk 22 in PRU colours photographed by the late Charles Brown and believed never before published* (RAF Museum).
Above *Inside the cockpit of Mk IX MH434 which is now owned by Ray Hanna* (Stuart Howe).

Above *The Battle of Britain Flight's Mk IIa, after being correctly repainted as* UO:T, *just after take-off at the Greenham Common air display in 1974* (Stuart Howe).

Below *Two-seater Mk 9 ML407 in the markings of No 485 (New Zealand) Squadron with whom it flew in 1944.*

Above *Mk 9 MH434 painted with Adrian Swire's initials as 'codes' prior to its purchase by Ray Hanna* (Stuart Howe).

Below *Cliff Robertson's Mk IX, MK923* (Stuart Howe).

Above *Hangar maintenance work on the Battle of Britain Flight's P6853 (Stuart Howe).*

Below *Ray Hanna prepares to take off in MH434.*

Since 1939 it had been accepted that the view from the Spitfire's cockpit was inadequate. Bulges added first to the canopy roof and then on its sides brought welcome improvements. Various types of rear-view mirrors were fitted, but the best answer was a teardrop-shaped, 'clear view all round canopy'. That required the cutting away and lowering of the rear fuselage and, inevitably, raising again the question of structural stength. Mid-1943 saw a Spitfire flying with these changes, but it was December 1944 before the new style canopies and fuselages were introduced onto the production line, mainly as 'Modification 963' applicable to the Mk XVI. Earlier substitution would have played havoc with Spitfire output. Teardrop canopy Spitfires served mostly in the post-war period by which time the whistle of the Merlin was being largely replaced by the growl of the Griffon.

Unquestionably, the major and almost inevitable change was the replacement of the Spitfire's Merlin with that engine's successor. Such a notion first arose in September 1939. The 1,700 hp Rolls-Royce Griffon engine was reckoned likely, even then, to give the fighter a top speed of well over 400 mph. But it was obvious that the Merlin was still in its infancy and making such a major change to the Spitfire during this critical period was deemed unwise. Just how much the Merlin had to offer was uncertain; in the event the answer was much indeed. The decision to put aside the Griffon, an engine based closely upon those which powered the S.6 racing seaplanes, was an intelligent one.

Heavier and longer, with cylinder banks protruding further than the Merlin's, the Griffon was not quite as easy to install in the Spitfire as at first seemed. Certainly its frontal dimensions were satisfactory, but its use required enlarged tail units to compensate for the enlarged nose. Because of the engine's power output the torque was considerable, for which reason five-bladed propellers or experimental counter-rotating propellers were fitted to most Griffon-engined Spitfires. Increased power had a profound effect upon general handling and whilst the ultimate Griffon Spitfires could attain 470 mph the sweetness of the Merlin Spitfires had gone. Flying very fast meant that the compressibility of the airflow over the wing could also bring handling problems which ultimately resulted in a completely redesigned Spitfire, the Spiteful.

The Griffon Spitfire scheme was resurrected in December 1940, although Rolls-Royce still preferred to stay with the Merlin. Official forecasts projected that a Griffon Spitfire would reach 430 mph at 23,500 ft and that a two-stage supercharger version would top 470 mph at 35,000 ft. Supermarine, playing safe, designed a six-cannon wing for a Griffon Spitfire, the Mk IV, which they hoped would fly in August 1941 and enter production at the end of that year. The engine programme slipped, but when in September 1941 the Fw 190 began fighting over France work was hastened and the prototype Griffon Spitfire flew on 27 November 1941. In December 1941 an order was placed for 100 Spitfire Vc airframes to be fitted with Griffons. Two-stage supercharger Griffon 61s would go into a new range of Spitfires, the Mk XX series, to enter production in July 1943.

On 8 August 1942 the first Griffon 61 Spitfire (designed from the outset to have

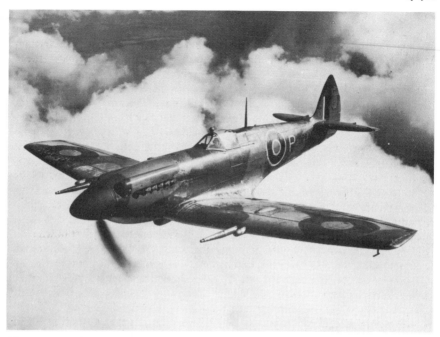

Above DP845 *began life as the first Griffon Spitfire, the Mk IV. Subsequently, with wings clipped and a Griffon suited to low-level operations, it served as the prototype Spitfire Mk XII.*

Below *Only two squadrons (Nos 41 and 91) operated Mk XIIs. Depicted here are* MB882 *and* MB858 *of 41 Squadron.*

a fighter-bomber role) first flew. Weighing around 9,000 lb, it nevertheless showed a top speed of 455 mph at 25,600 ft, reached 30,000 ft in 7.5 minutes, had a top rate of climb of 4,800 ft/min at 7,700 ft and a service ceiling of 42,800 ft: no mean performance, although operational equipment would have reduced these figures.

To help defeat Fw 190 fighter-bomber strikes on the south coast, it was decided that the first hundred Griffon Spitfires should have engines giving maximum power at low altitudes. Fifty, known as Mk XIIs, were ordered to be built by the end of the year. That was an impossible task and only five were built in that time scale, the first production example appearing in October 1942, its top speed being 396 mph at 38,600 ft.

As the first production Mk XII was being prepared for flight, an audacious move was undertaken by a group of officers of the Air Fighting Development Unit at Duxford. On their own initiative, and remembering the Spitfire III, they removed three square feet off each wing tip from Spitfire Vb, *AA937*, and plugged the tip end with wooden fairings. When the machine was first flown on 2 October 1942, the effect upon its performance was found to be quite dramatic. Very light ailerons and a fast rate of roll were coupled with greatly improved low level performance. Although it climbed more slowly, the clipped wing Spitfire remained fairly manoeuvrable to 30,000 ft.

When news of the venture reached the Assistant Chief of the Air Staff, responsible for aircraft development, he expressed his anger in splendid style to Duxford, ordering no more flying of *AA937* — except by the experts at Boscombe Down. Unless the ailerons were suitably modified, he claimed, the aircraft could

Clipping the wings of Spitfires much improved handling at low altitudes, and many were thus modified from 1943 onwards, like this Spitfire Vb of 316 City of Warsaw Polish Squadron (RAF Museum 5973–).

Above *Spitfire Vbs of 243 Squadron were among those which supported the Allied invasions of Sicily and Italy in the summer of 1943. Illustrated are tropicalized examples, some of which reverted to grey-green camouflage* (IWM).

Right *The Griffon-engined Supermarine 379 Spitfire F Mk XIV.*

be very dangerous to fly. Certainly Duxford's pilots had reported how easy it was for the machine to fly one wing low. Privately, the ACAS(T) expressed another view — that this was a very bright idea well worth pursuing! It took but a matter of days to officially decide that this was all a splendid idea and the following month 92 Squadron began operating clipped wing tip Spitfire LF Vbs. Orders were also given to start clipping the wing tips of Spitfire XIIs, by which time Fighter Command courageously admitted that the wing tips of one of their Spitfire IXs had also received a trim. Thousands of Spitfire IXs, almost every Mk XVI and indeed many other marks of Spitfires subsequently had their wing tips clipped in service and on production lines although no clipped Mk Vs were ever built. Clipping the Mk XII's wings not only improved low level handling, but also resulted in a top speed of 396 mph at 18,600 ft. With the emphasis on medium and high flying Spitfires remaining strong, an order was given on 10 April 1943 that all Spitfire Vs were to have their wing tips clipped, the necessary wooden tip fairings to be made locally. As they became available, engines with clipped impellors were also fitted to Mk Vs.

While the more aged Spitfires were being clipped Rolls-Royce had also come across a highly successful new line. Six Spitfire VIIIs had been allocated to them for Griffon 60 series development. Delivering over 2,000 hp, the wedding of this mighty engine to the Spitfire seemed certain to bring major problems. Instead, all went amazingly well, and in January 1943 soon after the first armed conversion flew it reached 445 mph at 25,000 ft. So impressive was its performance and general handling that in April 1943 — just as the first Mk XIIs were entering squadron service — the decision was made to order fifty Spitfires powered by the

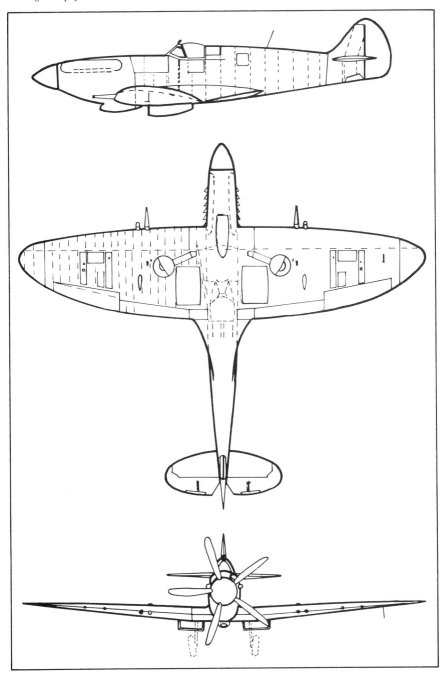

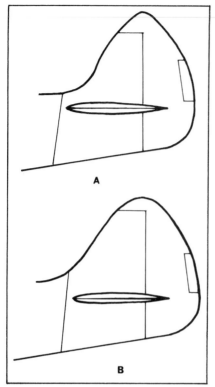

A

B

N: *Increased engine power resulted in modifications to the tails of Spitfires. 'A' shows the 'pointed' or broad chord rudder fitted to many Merlin 60, 70 and Packard Merlin Spitfires — also the Mk XII, first Griffon version to enter operational service. 'B' shows the type designed in September 1943 and fitted to Mk XIV, XVIII and 21 Spitfires fitted with Griffon engines.*

Spitfire F.XIV (Griffon 65) salient data

Wing span 36 ft 10 in. Length overall 32 ft 8 in. Height 11 ft 8½ in. Wing area 242 sq ft. Tare weight 6,376 lb, normal loaded weight 8,475 lb. Maximum speed FS — 439 mph TAS at 24,500 ft, time to 20,000 ft — 7 minutes, initial climb 4,500 fpm. Service ceiling 43,000 ft. Retractable tailwheel, undercarriage track 5 ft 8 ½ in. Fuel, top main tank — 36 gallons, bottom main tank — 48 gallons, 12.75 gall in each wing tank. Able to carry a 30, 45 or 90 gallon auxiliary drop tank. Propeller, Rotol five-blade Jablo R4.19/5F5/1 of 10 ft 5 in diameter.

2,035 hp Griffon 65. A longer nose contoured to contain the Griffon, five-bladed airscrew to help absorb its considerable torque and use its power, enlarged radiator boxes and increased area tail surfaces were virtually all that were needed.

Just as the Merlin 45 and 61 had so readily transformed earlier airframes, so the highly successful Griffon derivative arrived unexpectedly. The first operational example of this, the Spitfire Mk XIV, was delivered on 20 December 1943 and on 2 January 1944 No 610 Squadron received its first example. So immediately successful was the Mk XIV that another 400 were ordered in February 1944. Ultimately a family of Mk XIVs appeared, early examples having 'C' wings and later ones 'E' wings. The 'E' wings were a late war feature because the Air Staff thought that .50 in guns would be of little value in combat against heavily armoured aircraft. In the event, the Mk XIVs operated particularly against ground targets, the late-war photographing of which was undertaken by Spitfire FR XIVs fitted with 'teardrop-all-round view' canopies and a camera in the rear port side of the fuselage. In the summer of 1945, Spitfire XIVs were despatched to the Far East, but the squadrons were not ready to fight before hostilities ceased. In the war in northern Europe, Mk XIVs performed splendidly, so much so that in December 1944 it was decided to develop a sophisticated version, the 9,000 lb Mk XVIII which replaced the Mk XIV on production lines in March 1945.

All Mk XVIIIs had 'teardrop' canopies and 'E' armament, the strengthened undercarriage making the Mk XVIII well suited to carrying underwing loads including bombs and rockets. First came the F.Mk XVIII featuring a 62-gallon fuel tank in its rear fuselage. Following was the FR Mk XVIII which had two vertical cameras and one oblique camera in the aft section of the fuselage. These versions served after the war, in the Mediterranean and Far East areas. Quickly classed as obsolete, in May 1946, the F.XVIII was then replaced by its fighter reconnaissance successor.

When development of the Griffon Spitfire was decided upon, the intention was for it to have the two-stage Mk 61 type of engine. The third Griffon Spitfire had pointed wing tips emphasizing the notion that such Spitfires would be high fliers. By the time the first fully schemed example first flew, on 24 July 1943, radical future conflict trends were apparent for the first jet interceptor fighters were in being. For the present they could be operationally discounted. But with the RAF concentrating upon night bombing and increasing numbers of USAAF fighters arriving in Europe to escort their own bombers — a task which RAF Spitfire squadrons had undertaken although limited by range — the British fighters were increasingly switching to ground attack roles. Nevertheless, the Spitfire XXI, production Griffon 61 machine, was seen as a high altitude air superiority fighter. With a forecast top speed of around 470 mph, it was little wonder that 3,000 were ordered, and so radically different was this version expected to become that it was even given a new name, the Victor.

Unexpectedly successful was the F Mk XIV Griffon-engined Spitfire, of which RB140 was the first production example (RAF Museum 5986–14).

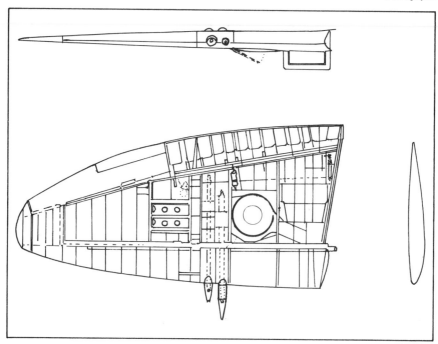

Designed in March 1944, the layout of the starboard mainplane of the Spitfire 21/22/24 shows the revised wing tip and provision for short-barrelled Mk V Hispano 20-mm cannon. The wing aerofoil section is also shown.

To cope with its engine of over 2,000 hp the aircraft had stronger, thicker skinned wings which included ailerons eight inches longer held in place by piano-type hinges. Strength during high speed flying needed attention for, in a dive, the aircraft would be flying extremely fast. Extending the ailerons meant wing tip modifications which ultimately added two square feet to the wing area and resulted in a more angular wing tip. Wider undercarriage track, stronger undercarriage legs, smart doors closing over the retracted wheels and a huge, 11 ft 7 in diameter five-blade propeller, made this a most pugnacious, powerful, noisy performer.

Partly because of the incorporation of so many new features — and not least the growling Griffon — the Mk XXI proved a disappointment. At 450 mph — slower than expected — lateral stability problems delayed the machine. Although the first production example flew on 15 March 1944, and delivery to aircraft storage commenced in September 1944, it was January 1945 before the first examples joined 91 Squadron. Part of the Coltishall fighter-bomber wing, they were employed against miniature submarines operating off Belgium.

So drastic was the cut in production when the war finished that only 120 Spitfire XXIs were built, all at the Swindon works, building being completed in

January 1946. Four Regular Air Force squadrons used Mk XXIs, the last example being retired in August 1947. At around this time the Air Ministry appears to have decreed the use of Arabic as opposed to Roman numerals to describe Spitfire marks.

Between March 1945 and February 1946 a batch of 259 Spitfire F.22s was delivered to the RAF. These had cut-down rear fuselages and teardrop canopies, but were otherwise largely similar to the Mk 21. Vibration in the aircraft was unacceptably high and before any were suitable for RAF use all the F.22s needed much modified fins to improve directional stability. These were similar to those produced for Supermarine's next fighter, the Spiteful. With the variety of tasks these later Spitfires might need to fulfil, it was little wonder that the Mk 22 had a 24-volt electrical system in place of the usual 12-volt. It was intended that the Mk 22s would serve as ground attack fighters, able to carry bombs and rockets, while their fighter cover flew overhead. But the Mk 22 was never acceptable to the RAF for its revised role, and instead many Mk 22s served in the post-war Royal Auxiliary Air Force as low and medium level interceptor fighters until sufficient jet fighters were available for Royal Auxiliary Air Force squadrons.

The ultimate Spitfire was the fully fledged ground attack Mk 24, two 33 gallon

Virtually last of the line, a Spitfire 22 (PK312) and, further away, its predecessor with the older style cabin, a Mk 21, LA217 (RAF Museum 6045–7).

A late production Spitfire, VN328 was laid down as a Mk 22, completed as a ground attack Mk 24, and was displayed at the 1950 RAeS Garden Party at Hatfield.

fuel tanks in the rear fuselage and short barrelled Hispano Mk Vs differentiating it from the Mk 22. Having been devised from the outset as a low-attack fighter the F.24 was much better suited to the purpose although its affinity to the Mk 22 was shown when 27 of those were modified into Mk 24s. First delivery of a Mk 24 took place from South Marston on 13 April 1946 against the background knowledge that a host of fighters more suited to ground attack were already serving. Only 80 Squadron in Germany operated Mk 24s, receiving its first examples in January 1948. During July 1949 the Squadron took its Mk 24s to Hong Kong. On 20 February 1948 Supermarine delivered *VN496*, their last production Spitfire, a Mk 24. In January 1952 the Spitfire was withdrawn from front line fighter duty as the last 80 Squadron machines left Hong Kong.

Thus, the outline of the Spitfire's development. Beyond that is the reality that the Spitfire may even now continue to change, and certainly it will not be retiring for a very long time. In the memories of millions, old and very young, Spitfires find a hallowed place. For myself, I still picture most vividly the scene at Duxford late summer 1938 when I first caught a glimpse of two Spitfires resting outside 19 Squadron's hangar. Alongside were the resident Gauntlets, which but a few weeks before were acceptably front line fighters. Suddenly they had become symbolic of a fading age. How excited we were when three of the very 'Secret' and camouflaged but oh-so-beautiful looking Spitfires from Duxford performed in public for the first time, at the opening of Cambridge Airport in October 1938. And there must be millions of people who will never forget the utterly unique whistle of the Spitfires passing by reminding us all that they were trying to protect us. How exhilarating, too, that distinctive sound as a squadron of Spitfires raced away, 'scrambled' for battle.

Surely, if you were around in wartime days, you will also remember the fun one had in trying to work out the mark number of a passing Spitfire. Often the differences between variants appeared none too great, while the long rumoured

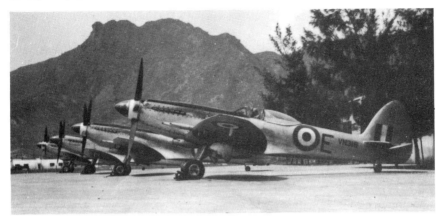

Last front line fighter-bomber Spitfires were the Mk 24s of 80 Squadron based at Hong Kong, four of which are shown here, VN318 *closest* (RAF Museum P7419).

Griffon Spitfires seemed so long in coming. Re-engining was an industry in itself. There was no reason why a Mk IX should not have a Packard Merlin, or a Mk V fly with the aid of a Merlin II, provided the balance and strength were adhered to. Hybrid Spitfires were and remain quite acceptable, which makes havoc of any attempt to produce the 'final word' on the question of production by mark numbers.

As for the sheer joy of watching a Spitfire in the hands of an ace performer, how can one ever forget the brilliance of Alex Henshaw and Jeffrey Quill? Their contribution as test pilots to the Spitfire's continuing success was enormous. How well, too, the nation came to know and acknowledge so many great Spitfire names — Douglas Bader, 'Paddy' Finucane, Johnnie Johnson, Mungo Park and many others, all of whom had in their teams the enormously brave and greatly talented. Top button undone, bright scarf flying, thumbs up and a grand smile all belied the cruel reality of battle. Immortalized, they most rightly and assuredly are, their images and those of their Spitfires being brightly woven into Sir Winston Churchill's momentous phrases, and superbly enshrined in Sir William Walton's grand tribute to 'The First of the Few'.

What other memories close in, as one of today's few Spitfires performs? Victory rolls on hot summer days, huge armadas mothering American Marauders, the 'trolley acc' in place, the rush on the 'Scramble!', that smell gone forever from a hangar of Spitfires, an inextricable scent mixing petrol, oil, metal, real leather, spent cordite and even man in his little enclosed cockpit!

Every September, as Battle of Britain Day is celebrated, such recollections must race through many an ageing mind recalling days of ghastly pathos and mingled with enormous pride. Dreams of times when one was immensely proud of being 'British', however badly the battle was going. Pride, yes, immense pride in achievement, that is what the nation felt towards the Spitfire and in return it fought brilliantly to keep us free.

Chapter 8
What shall we do with all these Spitfires?

Careful counting on 31 May 1945 revealed that the RAF held 5,864 Spitfires, 339 of them heading overseas and only 510 unsuitable for immediate use. Such figures are one measure of the part Spitfires played in the closing weeks of the conflict, at a time when RAF stocks totalled a staggering 55,469 aircraft. Among operational types, only the 3,408 Mosquitoes rivalled the Spitfire's pride of place. How the Spitfire force had grown: for on 30 June 1939, the nearest comparative date for which figures have survived, there were only nine Spitfire squadrons armed with 136 Mk Is and backed by 85 reserve aircraft.

What then, should and could be done with so many Spitfires? Many, with much war service, would inevitably be of little further military use. Those serving Allied Air Forces' squadrons, perhaps replacements for those aircraft, could be directly transferred to new air forces being formed by liberated European countries. Thus, the Belgians, Czechs, Dutch, French, Greeks and Norwegians would all inherit Spitfires within their defence forces — which was reckoned to be a favourable gesture towards future British trade deals. Regrettably, indeed disgracefully, the Poles, who had fought as well as any of our Allies, were being brutally deceived. The freedom for which they and the rest of civilized Europe had fought was being denied them. Flying mostly Mustangs at the end of the war, five Polish squadrons and RAF fighter squadrons retained them until Lend-Lease arrangements terminated their use at the end of 1946. Plans to retain and re-arm the Polish squadrons with Spitfire LF/HF 9s fell by the wayside and the distinguished Polish squadrons disbanded.

A few home-based RAF fighter squadrons were to re-arm, each with a mere eight Spitfires of the types available in most quantity, LF Mk 9s and 16s. Their most appropriate role was now the interception of low-flying or piston-engined intruders, jet fighters being left to tackle high fliers. Heavy fuel consumption and lack of sufficient tankage as yet prevented use of jets for low-level operations. However, following the 1946 Battle of Britain Day fly-past, Fighter Command suffered even more drastic pruning than expected, which left Spitfires in only two squadrons, Nos 41 and 63, in the front line, with four more giving training to the sizeable force of anti-aircraft batteries still very much part of our defences. At Keevil, No 61 Operational Training Unit trained aircrew for the RAF's low-flying fighter/reconnaissance Spitfire squadrons to be based in Germany and overseas.

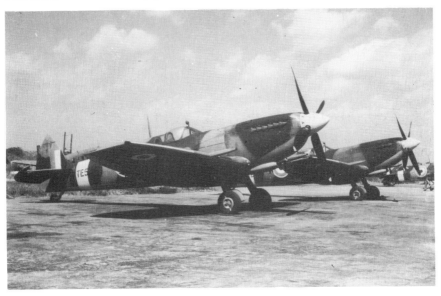

Above *What could be done after the war with so many surplus Spitfires? Mk 16 TE534 and its two companions shown here, headed for the delights of France.*

Below *The Royal Belgian Air Force made good use of Spitfire F XIVs, these being of the 2 eme Escadrille 'La Comete' with 'UR:S' closest (Amilpress).*

Sales to foreign and Commonwealth air forces

Wartime and post-war sales/supply of Spitfires to other nations (based on Air Ministry and Ministry of Supply statistics):
Australia 245 Vc, 251 F VIII, 159 HF VIII. *Belgium* 48 IX/XVI, 132 FR 14. *Canada* 10 plus? *Czechoslovakia* 76 LF IX/XVI. *Denmark* 36 HF IX, 3 PR XI. *Egypt* 12 Vc, 20 F.22. *Eire* 12 Seafire Mk III and 1 'T Mk IX'. *France* 70 Vb, 172 F IX. *Greece* 74 LF IX, 3 HF IX, 1 PR XI, 8 plus LF 16. *India* 150 F VIII, 10 'T.IX', 70 Mk XIV, ? 18s, ? PR 19s.

Israel 50 LX IX from Czechoslovakia, 30 LF IX from Italy, and additional uncertain quantity from various sources and a number ex-RAF. *Italy* 99 IX. *Netherlands* 54 F IX, 3 'T.IX', 4 PR XI. *Norway* 47 F IX, 3 PR XI. *Portugal* 15 Mk I, 50 Vb. *South Africa* 139 F IX. *Siam* 30 FR XIV. *Southern Rhodesia* 22 F. 22. *Sweden* 50 PR XIX. *Syria* 16 F.22. *Turkey* 3 Mk I, 33 LF IX, 2 XVI. *USA* 7 (?) Mk VII, 16 F IX, 8 PR XI. *USSR* 1,186 LF IX, 2 HF IX, 143 F Vc.

More Spitfires found a ready home in a new Auxiliary Air Force resurrected in mid-1946. After growing pains this reserve force began slowly equipping thirteen of its twenty squadrons with Spitfires in October 1946. Their intended role was to give top cover to Mosquito bombers, but when even the faster Griffon Spitfires were seen to be at operational risk plans were altered to make the entire RAuxAF a reconnaissance fighter/ground attack force. Modifying the Spitfire 22 for the latter task proving too complicated and expensive, the seven Auxiliary squadrons flying Spitfire LF 16s and three the Mk 21 like the other eleven squadrons, were now to be equipped with interceptor Mk 22s. Training Flights for the Griffon Spitfire squadrons mostly received four Spitfire F/FR 14s each. The force of Packard Merlin Spitfire Mk 16s was partly backed with British-built engines, which theoretically, could convert the aircraft into Mk 9s. The initial intention was to arm each RAuxAF squadron with nine Spitfires then double the quantity upon introduction of Griffon Spitfires, Mk 21, 22 and 24. Problems with the Mk 20-series played havoc with all schemes, and even the idea of having two German-based ground attack Spitfire 24 squadrons (Nos 33 and 80) was halved.

July 1948 saw the introduction of Meteors into the Auxiliary force, September 1948 bringing the Vampire. On 1 February 1949 the RAuxAF was placed under front line Fighter Command control at which time its squadrons held 221 Spitfires — 94, Mk 22s; 53, Mk 16s; 32, FR 14s; 23, F 14s; and 19, F 21s. By the end of March 1949 all the Spitfire 14s and 16s had been withdrawn leaving the squadrons equipped with 22 Mk 21s and 120 Mk 22s. A few days later it was decided to replace them all with jet fighters, after selected airfields had been prepared. Not until mid-1951, though, were the F 22s finally phased out, 603, 607, 611 and 612 Squadrons being the last to retain the type.

In the Middle East and Mediterranean area 1947-48 was to see four squadrons flying Mk 9s, one at least with Mk 18s and one using Mk 22s, but there the Mustang squadrons would re-arm with Tempest VIs. Three squadrons of Mk 16s earmarked for the forces of occupation in Japan were never needed. For India three squadrons — one using sixteen F 14s manned and flown by the Royal Indian

Above *The Americans made use of a moderate number of Spitfire Vs, sixteen IXs, and for photo-reconnaissance employed PR XIs like MB955. This aircraft was transferred to the 8th Air Force on 5 December 1943, and is shown here wearing its number on the fin, USAAF style.*

Below *Three post-war Spitfire LF IXs, the nearest (NH533) fitted with a 90-gallon slipper tank nestling around its late production tropical air filter. Black spinners and no rear fuselage band were typical of Spitfires in Egypt post-war.*

Air Force, one using FR 14s and one, FR 18s — were planned. India's demand for freedom soon altered such notions, but the Indians nevertheless acquired Spitfires for their own air force.

The RAF had planned to have 22 squadrons of General Purpose Spitfire fighters in March 1947, only nine a year later. Available stock would replace likely losses during two months of warfare. Already, the atomic age had altered all forecasting. After many complex plans, related mainly to financial restraint and not military desire, jet production was reduced and a further scheme reinstated sixteen Spitfire squadrons for spring 1947. The final outcome was that for nearly five years after the war, over ten years all told, Spitfires played a major role in home defence. The last bastion of Spitfires in Britain was a group of five Civilian Anti-Aircraft Co-operation Units established in 1951 when the anti-aircraft support squadrons disbanded. For the next three years Spitfires were the main equipment of the civilian-manned units at Hornchurch, Little Snoring/Langham, Exeter, Llandow and Llanbedr. When the second and fourth of these combined at Exeter, their Mk 21 Spitfires were retired in favour of Mk 16s, themselves relinquished in 1954.

It was four of those (*RW352, SL574, TE358* and *TE456*) which in 1955 acquired normal wing tips, and guns, for their part in the filming at Kenley of *Reach for the Sky*, the story of Douglas Bader's life. By that time a far more

Left *In Britain, the main user of the LF 16e was the Royal Auxiliary Air Force. Others served in a wide variety of units, RW396 for instance as 'F:JWL' of the Central Gunnery School at Leconfield.*

Below left *Few Spitfires served long enough with the RAuxAF to acquire small-size squadron markings on their cowlings. Initially they had letters in the Reserve Command sequence — 'RAR' here signifying 611 Squadron, with Mk 22, PK669, closest to the camera (RAF Museum P015075).*

Below *TE120, an LF 16 with old-style cockpit, survived long enough to acquire post-war roundels, and is seen here at the 1950 RAF Display.*

Above *Like the Irish Air Corps, the Belgian civilian-operated Spitfire 9s of COGEA have also been eagerly purchased by private buyers. OO-ARE's task, like those of its companions, was mainly target towing and operating as a target aircraft.*

Below *Looking every inch a splendid Spitfire, Mk 16 TB308 during its gate-guarding days.*

important milestone in the Spitfire story had been passed for on 1 April 1954 it had fallen to Squadron Leader William Proctor Swaby in Spitfire PR 19 *PS888* of 81 Squadron to fly the last front-line operational sortie by a Spitfire — a photo-reconnaissance sortie over Malaya.

At the close of 1954 there were only three regularly active RAF Spitfires in Britain, all PR 19s serving with the civilian-operated Temperature and Humidity (THUM) flight operated from Hooton Park and later Woodvale by Short Bros & Harland. Their task was the gathering of meteorological data for the Central Forecasting Office at Dunstable. Over 4,000 sorties were made by these Spitfires before they retired in June 1957.

Yearly official totals of Spitfires delivered to the RAF

1939	1940	1941	1942	1943	1944	1945	TOTAL
434	1,246	2,518	4,134	4,276	4,916	2,627	20,151

Spitfires on Royal Air Force charge, 29 April 1948

Still being broken down: Mk Va — 1, Mk Vc/a — 2, Mk Vb —10, Mk Vc — 4
Spitfires in RAuxAF Day Reserve Fighter Squadrons:
UE = Usual Establishment (authorized strength), Str = Actual strength

	F14		FR14		LF16		F21		F22	
	UE	Str	UE	Str	UE	Str	UE	Str	UE	Str
Operational	24	17	—	20	32	43	24	21	56	3
Training flights	6	9	6	16	20	17	—	—	42	—

Of the 1,050 LF Mk 16s ordered, 442 were still effective aircraft, 83 of them being used in Flying Training Command. Also remaining effective were 84 Mk 21s, 252 Mk 22s and 86 Mk 24s (15 in BAFO). Of the 527 F Mk 14s ordered, and the 430 FR 14s, 296 were still effective aircraft.

Breakdown of the RAF's Mk 9 and 14 series showed:

	Already struck off charge in UK	Already struck off charge overseas
LF 9	1,152	823
F 9	380	599
HF 9	107	63
F 14	179	137 + 38 sold abroad
FR 14	70	207 + 7 sold abroad

Direct Mk 9 sales/disposal:
LF 9 — 1,186 to USSR, 172 to France.
F 9 — 1 from the RAF to Royal Navy, 61 to Dominions, 16 to USAAF, 61 to France, 83 to other countries.
HF 9 — 2 to USSR, 19 to France, 38 to Dominions.
By 30 September 1948 total effective RAF Spitfire strength had fallen to:
Mk 16 — 411, Mk F 18 — 84, Mk FR 18 — 118, Mk PR 19 — 99, Mk F 21 — 82, Mk F 22 — 251, Mk F 24 — 85. Total held 1,130 (ie, excluding other aircraft in servicing units, being broken down or held for exhibition purposes)

A decade has passed, and still they practice Air Drill! Spitfire 22s demonstrate at the 1950 RAF Display, the last major public engagement for the Spitfire.

Spitfire production

Widespread production sources, pattern aircraft for sub-contractors' use, extensive modification programmes, changes during RAF service, all combine to make it extremely difficult to establish the precise numbers of Spitfires produced, fully assembled and flown. It is little wonder that so many production lists have appeared. The following listing is believed to be accurate:

Mk 1 1,569	*Mk Vc* 2,459	*PR Mk X* 16	*PR Mk XIX* 225
Mk II 921	*'PR Mk V/F'* 15	*PR Mk XI* 471	*Mk 21* 120
Mk III 2	*Mk VI* 100	*Mk XII* 100	*Mk 22* 287
PR Mk IV 229	*Mk VII* 140	*Mk XIV* 957	*Mk 24* 54
Mk Va 94	*Mk VIII* 1,652	*Mk XVI* 1,054	
Mk Vb 3,925	*Mk IX* 5,656	*Mk XVIII* 300	

Additional to these were eight prototypes — *K5054*; a Mk IV/XII; a Mk XX/21; a Mk 21; a Mk 22; a Mk XIX and a Mk 21 completed as the Seafire 45 prototype. A Mk V was also completed as the Seafire prototype, but that aircraft type lies beyond this volume devoted to the Spitfire.

Spitfires serving in the Royal Auxiliary Air Force 1949

UE = Usual Establishment, Str = Actual strength

	F 14		FR 14		LF 16		F 21		F22	
	UE	Str	UE	Str	UE	Str	UE	Str	UE	Str
27 January 1949 Operational	—	13	—	23	32	38	24	15	72	69
Training	—	10	—	8	16	15	12	4	36	25
31 March 1949 Operational	—	—	—	—	—	—	24	18	72	94
Training	—	—	—	—	—	—	12	4	36	26
30 June 1949 Operational	—	—	—	—	—	—	24	7	72	22
Training	—	—	—	—	—	—	12	4	36	22

Chapter 9
Going abroad

Foreign interest in acquiring Spitfires was evident as soon as the prototype made its mark despite the secrecy surrounding it. Eventually the Foreign Office approved Spitfire sales to twelve countries, with France foremost. Contracts with Greece, Portugal and Turkey were in the offing when the Second World War broke out, but a contract with no longer friendly Estonia had by then been cancelled. As Poland fell, a Spitfire intended for its air force was hurriedly diverted to Turkey which received another two in a 'goodwill gesture' late in 1940. One Spitfire delivered to the French was captured at Orleans in 1940 by the Germans. Otherwise, Spitfires remained firmly in British hands until 1942, then in November eighteen Mk Is were released to Portugal, Britain's oldest ally. A year later, after the Azores Agreement whereby Coastal Command operated from Portuguese bases, 33 Mk Vbs were passed to Portugal which received more Mk Vs later. Political forces were also instrumental in Turkey having Mk Vs in 1944, and more after the war, and also the equipment of a Royal Egyptian Air Force squadron with Mk Vcs in 1942.

By that time, as part of a deal related to the British getting Merlin-engined Mustangs, agreement was reached for the provision of up to 600 Spitfires for USAAF Fighter Groups in Europe. Transfer of Spitfires to the Americans in Britain commenced in mid-1942 and soon the 31st Fighter Group and then the 52nd Fighter Group equipped with Mk Vbs. Both Groups supported early B-17 operations, and flew fighter sweeps over France. The three ex-RAF Eagle Squadrons, also flying Spitfires and forming the 4th Fighter Group soon joined in these operations. Further Mk Vs were drafted into the 67th Observation Group at Membury which used them into 1944.

The 31st and 52nd Groups had been posted in November 1942 to north-west Africa to support the Operation Torch landings. By that time they were largely using tropicalized Mk Vcs, which were replaced in 1943 by Spitfire VIIIs and IXs with which the Americans fought in the Sicilian and Italian campaigns until March 1944 when the Spitfires were replaced.

Two Greek squadrons, ten South African Air Force squadrons, a 'free' Italian group and a Yugoslav squadron also operated in the Mediterranean Theatre, but the biggest overseas contingent was to be found in the USSR which received great quantities of Allied aircraft. From early 1943 Mk Vbs began to be passed to the

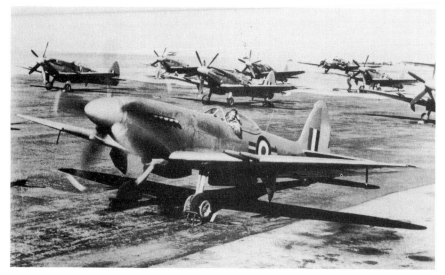

Syria and the Rhodesian Air Force purchased Spitfire F 22s. Two of the latter survived for a long while, but one restored to flying crashed. The fate of the other is not known for certain (Royal Rhodesian Air Force photograph).

Russians through Iraq. Eventually the USSR, expressing little gratitude for the aid, received 1,188 of the superlative Spitfire IXs. What use they made of them, if any, remains uncertain, but it seems certain that the USSR did not make as much use of them as it could have done. Maybe their vast superiority over any Russian aircraft was politically unacceptable!

All the British Dominions answered the battle call, in strength and from the very start. In the case of Australia two of its squadrons formed in the UK, 452 and 457, were posted home in 1942 along with the famous British No 54 Squadron. Formed then into No 1 Fighter Wing they were supplied with 245 Mk Vcs for home defence. Replacement in the form of Spitfire VIIIs came in 1944, then 452 and 457 Squadrons moved into New Guinea after which two new squadrons, 548 and 549, using some of the MK VIIIs, formed in Australia to replace them. Supplies also allowed another two Mk VIII squadrons, Nos 79 and 85, to operate in New Guinea.

During the war 656 Spitfires were taken on charge by the Royal Australian Air Force. Included were Mk Vcs re-registered *A58-1* to *A-58-185* (*A58-1*, for instance, was one of the first six delivered in August 1942, having been *AR510*), and *A58-200-259*. The remainder were Mk VIIIs, except for six PR XIs fitted at random into the Mk VIII serial ranges, *A58-300* to *A58-550*, *A58-600* to *A58-757*. The last Spitfire reached Australia in June 1945.

It was late 1944 when the Indian Air Force began flying Mk Vcs, and early 1945 when Mk VIIIs were introduced into its squadrons. The surfeit of Spitfires in the

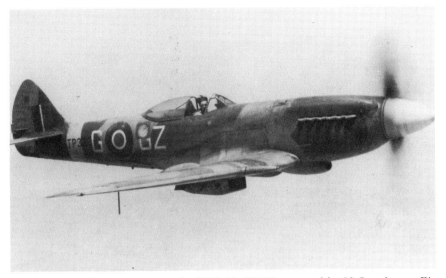

Most aggressive was the Griffon-engined Mk 18. TP330 was used by 32 Squadron at Ein Shemer (RAF Museum P12096).

Far East after the war allowed the Indians to have more Spitfires, particularly Mk 9s and 14s.

Post-war delivery of Spitfires to other countries included surplus Mk 22s to Syria and Southern Rhodesia, Mk 14s to Thailand, Mk 9s to Italy and a strange sale of twelve Seafire IIIs and a Spitfire 'T 9' to the Irish Air Corps, whose aircraft after years of service are still very much alive though now in new ownership.

Without doubt, the most secretive Spitfire operators in the post-war world have been the Israelis. On 15 May 1948 the British Palestinian Mandate ended, after six months of increasingly bitter conflict between Arab and Jew, with the British caught in the cross-fire and supported by ground strafing Spitfires. On the day the Mandate ended two Egyptian Spitfire LF 9s attempted to bomb and strafe Tel Aviv, where a defending gunner brought down one of them by pouring shots into its coolant tank. Two RAF squadrons, 32 and 208, equipped with Spitfire FR 18s, were still in Palestine at Ramat David, covering the British withdrawal. Early on 22 May 1948, a low flying unidentified Spitfire IX circled the camp before dropping two bombs which set ablaze two of 32 Squadron's Spitfires. Then it strafed others before fleeing ahead of four scrambled Mk 18s of 208 Squadron.

Two hours later another three Spitfires struck, this time bombing a hangar, setting a Dakota on fire and damaging more grounded Spitfires. Alert already, the RAF Spitfires were quickly scrambled and soon destroyed one of the attackers in the first intended Spitfire-versus-Spitfire combats. Another smashed into the desert while the third fell to ground fire. Next day the Egyptians announced a 'regrettable navigational error'.

The Israeli Air Force was not yet ready for a fight. Indeed, the United Nations had placed an embargo on the supply of arms to Israel. But helped by generous, maybe foolish Americans, and by scavenging the plentiful aircraft dumps in the Middle East, the Israelies, by skill and hard endeavour, gathered together an air force, a high proportion of which came from the most unlikely source, Czechoslovakia. Presumably the supply to Israel of Czech-built Me 109s and over thirty Spitfire LF 9s was to assist in destabilization of the area. But the Jews, smarter than the Czech government, soon had Spitfires facing the Arab nations and Soviet half-friends.

Continuing attacks by the Egyptian Air Force on the new Israel were embarrassing to Britain because under its twenty-year treaty, rights were held to station forces in the Canal Zone. In exchange, Britain would aid Egyptian forces if they were attacked — and the Egyptians were being intercepted by Spitfires of the new Israeli air force.

Keeping an eye on the delicate, fluid situation, was far from easy especially as RAF squadrons in the Canal Zone were ordered to make sure not to cross Israeli borders. On 7 January 1949 among the observers was a flight of four Spitfire FR 18s of 208 Squadron and when none of them returned there was no mean alarm. Tempest fighters were sent to investigate and near the border suddenly found themselves confronted by Spitfires of the Israel Defence Force — which promptly shot one down.

It later transpired that ground fire at the border brought down a Spitfire, and, when the others circled to investigate, Israeli Spitfire 9s swept down upon them. All four fell in Egyptian territory, but by the time British salvage teams reached the wrecks they all had been most effectively scavenged by people with Jewish connections...

Apart from the Czech Spitfires, the Israelies also bought from the Italians once the United Nation arms embargo was lifted. By the mid-1950s the Israeli air force was getting more up-to-date equipment. In famed Jewish style Israel did not waste its Spitfires but promptly sold thirty of the best LF 9s and 16s to the Burmese who urgently wanted some for anti-terrorist operations. Flown out by Britons and over Arab territory, they bore Burmese markings. Israeli agents made certain that the Arabs believed the Spitfires had come directly from Britain — until the truth emerged and the Arabs refused to allow the transit flights. Disposal had now to be by a northern route, over Turkey, Persia and India, and was completed by the end of the year. Like so many other Israeli aircraft, Spitfire disposal brought them into the limelight. Enthusiasts in recent years have come to hear of ageing machines languishing in the sunshine as a kibbutzean trophy, some of them being Israeli Spitfires. Recently a few have come home where, hopefully, they will be restored to full health.

Chapter 10
Can I still come close to a Spitfire?

Where indeed can one still come face to face with a Spitfire? The answer is, in many parts of the world. So numerous were Spitfires in their prime that examples remain widely dispersed, but luckily concentrated in Britain. In seas around Europe many a Spitfire rests, albeit it much devoured by salt and sea. In freshwater lakes and rivers, smashed almost beyond recognition in fields and upon hillsides and doubtless hidden by jungle or sand lie more yet to be discovered, and probably scarcely worth the effort except from a safety viewpoint, a desire to give a known resting place or to acquire a still usable Spitfire component.

Apart from such relics of glory, items of sorrow, there are many Spitfires in amazingly fine health. They range through well-cared for museum items, gate-guardians whose value is such that they must soon surely be given more comfortable homes, Spitfires that languish in none too good state and garish colours, examples being restored by proud owners, and, most exotic of all, the few that still roar through their element and are extremely expensive, demanding, valuable items to maintain. Where does one find them? Some are readily found, others are tucked away and almost impossible to view without the owner unlocking the aircraft's shelter. A Spitfire is a valuable commodity, so such a viewpoint is quite understandable. The precise state of many remaining Spitfires is likely to change much in their fiftieth anniversary year, and hopefully more surviving examples may be located and others fully restored.

It would be pleasing to suggest that the first place to seek a Spitfire would be its birthplace, but there is only one at Southampton. A better place to start would be in London. On a hallowed site at Hendon from which some of the world's first aviators took to the air not long after flying in Britain commenced, stands the Royal Air Force Museum. Admission is free, opening times are 10:00 to 18:00 daily and 14:00 to 18:00 on Sundays, and two Spitfires are easy to find. *K9942* (alias *8383M*), a Mk I, is very special for it is the oldest remaining Spitfire, having joined the RAF in April 1939 flying first with 72 Squadron at Church Fenton and later at Drem, and then Acklington. During patrols covering the BEF withdrawal from France *K9942* was active from Gravesend. A wheels-up landing on 5 June 1940 deprived it of Battle of Britain service. The aircraft went to 7 OTU in August 1940 (the unit which became 57 OTU) and remained there until February 1942. *K9942* then had a major overhaul before in April 1943 it briefly returned to active

Top *The oldest surviving Spitfire is presently in sombre tones and can be viewed in the RAF Museum — in 72 Squadron's pre-war colours.*

Above *There was a time when Londoners, in the street, were reminded of Spitfires and the Battle of Britain. K9942 as 'RN:V' sits, in 1959, outside the MOD Building in Whitehall.*

service, at 53 OTU Kirton-in-Lindsey. On 22 October 1943 it was withdrawn and held in storage successively at 33, 82, 52 and 58 Maintenance Units before becoming a 71 MU Bicester display aircraft. On 9 November 1971 it was placed at Hendon and wears pre-war 72 Squadron markings.

PK724 placed nearby, provides a good contrast since it is a Mk 24 whose Griffon engine is open to view. *PK724*'s entire life was spent in factory or Aircraft Storage Units. With only a few flying hours it was grounded as *7288M*. After guarding the entrance to Brize Norton and then Gaydon, February 1970 saw it join Finningley's exhibition collection. At this RAF station it was restored to its original colours and moved to Hendon, where it was installed on 2 April 1971.

X4590, another Mk I, is aptly positioned in the nearby Battle of Britain Museum. Delivered to the RAF on 22 September 1940 it was issued early in October 1940 to 609 Squadron at Warmwell from where, in the hands of Pilot Officer S. J. Hill, *X4590* had a share in the destruction of a Ju 88. On 24 February 1941 it is officially listed as passing to 66 Squadron at Exeter, then was used from April 1941 by 57 OTU. In July 1941 303 (Polish) Squadron at Speke briefly used the machine before it underwent a complete overhaul by Scottish Aviation, part of the Civilian Repair Organization, prior to storage at 37 MU Burtonwood. February 1942 witnessed its delivery to 53 OTU in whose hands a flying accident on 4 October 1943 resulted in *X4590* returning again for 'RIW' (Repair in Works) after which, in unairworthy state it went to 3 MU Milton for long term storage and eventual use as a display aircraft. A stay at Cosford Museum preceded its 1978 arrival at Hendon where it is displayed as *'PR:F'* of 609 Squadron.

While you are in London, the next Spitfire to view could well be another Mk Ia, *P9444*, in the South Kensington Science Museum's third floor National Aeronautical Collection (open daily from 10:00 to 18:00 and on Sundays between 12:30 and 18:00). *P9444* was first used by RAE Farnborough from April 1940 until late May. Via 6 MU Brize Norton it reached 72 Squadron early in June. Badly damaged in a crash landing, it was placed in civilian repair hands. Its active service resumed at 58 OTU in July 1941, where it served until May 1942. Following further overhaul and repair, *P9444* was operated by 61 OTU from August 1942 to January 1943. Further civilian repair and storage followed before *P9444* served with 53 OTU from May to November 1943. Then its active days ceased as it was shuffled among storage units before it was chosen for display purposes on 28 August 1949. After being painted to resemble *'RN:D'* in 1940's style, the aircraft commenced residence at South Kensington in 1963. There, it is one of the few Spitfires that one can touch — just!

Close by in the museum — in a dark corner and on no account to be missed is the magnificent Schneider Trophy, won outright by Britain and now resting between the floats of the Supermarine S.6B *S1595*, the 1931 Schneider Trophy competitor. In the Science Museum one can examine all the exhibits very closely. All are, of course, in splendid condition. As in many museums, you will need a wide angle lens and at least a 200 ASA film if you want to take worthwhile photographs.

Completing London's collection of Spitfires is Mk Ia *R6915* finished in 1943 style markings. Of the capital's Spitfires this is the most distinguished. After joining 609 Squadron in late July 1940 at Middle Wallop, it was being flown by Pilot Officer N. Agazarian when he shot down a Bf 109 and a He 111, and by Flying Officer J. Dundas when it destroyed a Bf 110 — if the entries in 609 Squadron's records are correct. In October 1940 *R6915* retired for modifications and repairs before joining 602 Squadron at Prestwick late January 1941. In July 1941 it commenced service with 61 OTU, passing to 57 OTU with whom it

Above *An elderly, distinguished Spitfire Ia, R6915, still hangs in the Imperial War Museum in London.*

Below *A Spitfire 21 (LA226) fitted with contra-props. These counteracted the engine's torque.*

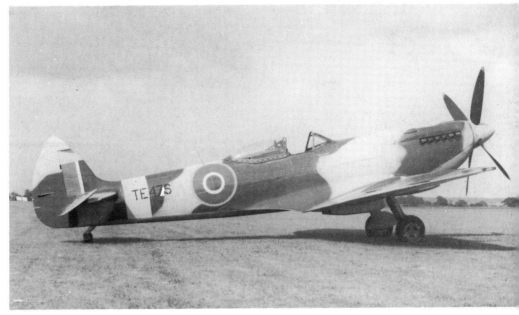

TE476, *a Mk 16, has guarded Northolt's gate for many years, but it is probably better known as a member of the embryo Battle of Britain Memorial Flight.*

operated between June and December 1943. Early in 1944 it briefly saw naval service before being placed in storage prior to joining the Imperial War Museum's collection in August 1946. Its colours, incidentally, are authentic.

At RAF Bentley Priory, Middlesex, for long HQ Fighter Command, is Spitfire LF 16 *SL574* used by the Empire Air Armament School, Manby, between September 1947 and July 1949 and then by the Central Gunnery School, Leconfield, before entering storage at 29 MU High Ercall in November 1949. From April to October 1951 *SL574* served at No 103 Flying Refresher School. Then in October 1953 the aircraft was posted to 3 CAACU, Exeter, where it operated until June 1956. As '*QV:R*' it had a part in the film *Reach for the Sky*. During March 1957 *SL574* began a period of use as an exhibition aircraft before being restored to airworthiness for 11 Group Communications Flight. Based then at Martlesham Heath, it was a participant in Battle of Britain commemoration flights until involved in a wheels-up landing on 28 May 1959 when it needed considerable repair. By this time airworthy RAF Spitfires were a rare commodity, and *SL574* was soon flying again. On 21 September 1959 over South London, Air Vice-Marshal H. J. Maguire had to make an emergency landing on a playing field at Bromley, Kent, as engine failure overtook *SL574*. Beyond repair for flying, the Spitfire found a home to be proud of, Bentley Priory, in November 1961. There, apart from refurbishing and a background role in *The Battle of Britain* film, it has remained, and carries the letters '*AZ:B*' of 234 Squadron.

Famed fighter station Biggin Hill currently has two grounded Spitfires, a Mk 16 *SL674*, and a Mk 21, *LA 226*, the latter being on loan from Vickers and possibly even by now withdrawn. The Mk 16 joined the RAF in July 1945 then between April and October 1946, served at 17 OTU. After storage at 6 MU Brize Norton it flew with 501 (County of Gloucester) Squadron between August 1947 and April 1949. Then 612 (County of Aberdeen) Squadron received it, the aircraft not retiring until July 1951 and it was thus one of the last Mk 16s in squadron hands. *SL674* flew into Biggin Hill on 11 September 1954 as part of that year's Battle of Britain display.

LA226 is an interesting Mk 21 in that it was one of the few to fly operationally. Delivered to 91 Squadron at Ludham, Norfolk, on 7 March 1945, it flew several operational sorties directed against small submarines operating off Belgium. Between January 1946 and December 1947 it was on the strength of 122 Squadron then based at Dalcross. Storage followed, *LA226* was refurbished and in October 1951 it joined No 3 Civilian Anti-Aircraft Co-operation Unit, Exeter, where it retired in November 1953 to become *7119M*. Via 2224 ATC Squadron at Albrighton, Staffordshire, and Cosford, *LA226* reached Little Rissington in February 1958 and was there restored and camouflaged. Earmarked for possible use in *The Battle of Britain* film, it went to Henlow in 1967, after which it passed into the hands of Vickers Ltd who displayed it at their Swindon works at South Marston. Recently on loan to Biggin Hill, it is due to return to Swindon.

Spitfire LF 16 *TE476* guards the gates of RAF Northolt. After a sheltered life, *TE476* was used by No 1 Civilian Anti-Aircraft Co-operation Unit, Hornchurch, between July 1951 and September 1956. Then it was prepared for exhibition before it was earmarked for 11 Group display flight in March 1958. Shortly thereafter 11 Group moved from North Weald to Martlesham Heath and became '11 Group Communications Flight', forerunner of The Battle of Britain Memorial Flight. January 1960 saw *TE476* again grounded and then placed on guard at Neatishead Radar Station, Norfolk. There it resided until 1967 when it was refurbished prior to taking up its present employment.

RAF Uxbridge also has a Spitfire, a Mk 16, *RW382*, pedestal mounted. Its active career began in April 1947 with 604 Squadron, Hendon, who retired it in April 1950 after moving to North Weald. In 1951 it joined No 3 Civilian Anti-Aircraft Co-operation Unit, Exeter but in the autumn of that year it was posted to the Fighter Control School at Middle Wallop and remained there until July 1953. From storage, it was sent to Church Fenton in November 1955, and to Leconfield four years later by which time its identity had changed to 'pseudo — *RW729*'. During later refurbishing it was restored to its rightful identity and in April 1973 went to Uxbridge.

If you should decide to search beyond London for Spitfires then surely the best place to start must be Southampton, the Spitfire's birthplace, which, naturally, proudly honours one of its greatest offspring. In Albert Road South is the Southampton Hall of Aviation housing the R. J. Mitchell Museum and much more. Prominently displayed is the Supermarine S. 6A racer, *N248* (which figured in the film *The First of the Few* as *S1596*), a Sandringham flying-boat and a

Spitfire F.24, *PK683*, which served in the Far East. In August 1950 it joined 80 Squadron in Hong Kong, then in July 1951 was transferred to the Singapore Auxiliary Air Force. Damaged in a flying accident the following February, it was then grounded as *715OM* and, wearing garish camouflage and the letters '*QV:A*', was placed at Changi's gate. In 1970 it was brought home for restoration at Bicester, and then stored before being placed in the new museum.

It is surprising that in the whole of Hampshire the Spitfire's ancestral home, only one example resides permanently. It would surely have been fitting to have placed the first prototype in a museum at Eastleigh by the Itchen, but *K5054* was wrecked at the start of the war when it overturned on landing at Farnborough the day after the war started.

At Duxford, Cambridgeshire, where the Spitfire's service career began, the airfield is now in the hands of the Imperial War Museum. The site is remarkably little changed since those days although upkeep costs have forced a tourist look upon what was always a spartan station. Nevertheless, one can still readily accept that a putteed airman may appear around the next corner hotly pursued by a stylish Station Warrant Officer! Rather surprisingly there is as yet little particular commemoration of the former RAF station's momentous link with the Spitfire, although memories of those halcyon days are still plentiful among many living in the area and many of whose intimate connections with pre-war 19 Squadron conflict with the usual written accounts. That even extends to the arrival date of the first Spitfire, which the locals all maintain was on a quiet Saturday prior to the official Tuesday! In August 1985 Duxford acquired a £35,000 plastic replica of Johnnie Johnson's Spitfire IX. Made by Specialised Mouldings of Huntingdon, Cambridgeshire, it is a very realistic reproduction.

What else you see of the Spitfire at Duxford will come by chance. Through much of 1985 Ray Hanna, the one-time 'Red Arrows' leader who owns the superbly kept Mk IX *MH434 'ZD:B'*, had the sorrow of seeing it engineless at Duxford, the powerplant needing drastic attention. Duxford is also the base for the British Aerial Museum of Flying Military Aircraft whose contingent seems likely to include Spitfires.

RAF Wittering is now (most illogically) part of Cambridgeshire, but the county's acquisition of a highly distinguished RAF station is something to be proud of. Wittering's No 1 Squadron was, of course, the first to fly Harriers, and is one of the few squadrons to possess one of its own aircraft from long ago. A Spitfire 21 *LA255*, it was received late June 1945 and flown from Tangmere for about a year before being written off on 13 November 1947 and becoming *649OM*. For years it squatted at Cardington in sorrowful state but then after refurbishment in 1964 it was released to No 1 Squadron at West Raynham. When the Squadron moved to Wittering, it carried along the coveted trophy. Apart from brief spells away, and time indoors or for refurbishing, *LA255* as '*JX:U*' has long been visible from the A1 road, in front of No 1 Squadron's hangar.

East Anglia currently possesses only two other Spitfires. Worthy of much better treatment is the clipped wing Spitfire Vb *EP120* sitting by RAF Wattisham's entrance as '*QV:H.*' Taken on charge in May 1942, it joined 501

Above *Travel along the A1 and pass RAF Wittering and you may have a glimpse of No 1 Squadron's Spitfire 21, LA255.*

Below *In a smart pale blue finish, Mk XVI, SL542, slipped into Duxford during the 1955 Battle of Britain display.*

Above *Running up the engine of* MH434 *prior to take-off.*

Below P6853 *in the Battle of Britain Flight hangar with access panels removed* (Stuart Howe).

Above *Another of the Mk IXs used in* The Battle of Britain *film* (Spitfire Productions Ltd).

Below *Spitfire LF 16 TE148 seen at Finningley in 1968 wearing spurious 488 Squadron markings — 488 only operated Beaufighters and Mosquitoes.*

Above *Another LF 16, RW382, on show at Leconfield in 1970.*

Below *An Israeli LF 16 now preserved at the Israeli Air Force Museum and photographed in civil markings at Beersheba in 1980* (Stuart Howe).

Above *Spitfire Mk 22 PK624 sheltering beneath the trees as gate guardian at Abingdon.*

Below *By contrast, and more difficult to photograph satisfactorily, here is the most distinguished surviving Spitfire of all, No 609 Squadron's Mk Ia R6915 which saw active service from 1940 to 1944. It is now hanging in the Imperial War Museum and must be a sight to inspire everyone (Stuart Howe).*

Camouflaged, and marked 'SH:N' to portray a 64 Squadron aircraft, SL542 *was to be seen, grounded, at Duxford in 1960.*

Squadron early in June to participate in patrols and sweeps, and operated during the Dieppe raid of 19 August 1942. Early in September 1942 it moved to 19 Squadron (hence its present coding) in 10 Group and in April 1943 joined No 402 (Canadian) Squadron at Kenley. An accident on 12 February 1944 required major attention before *EP120* joined 53 OTU in October 1944. In April 1945 it was grounded after its busy career. Used later for airframe training purposes at St Athan, it made its way via the gates of Wilmslow and Bircham Newton to Boulmer where, in 1964, it was carefully restored by an enthusiastic group led by Senior Technician J. Ayling. Since the late 1960s *EP120* has reminded entrants to Wattisham of the good things that many have missed!

Only one other 'Spitfire' resides in Suffolk, and that is one of the ground-only replicas built for the Battle of Britain film. Marked *P9390* and '*KL:B*', it can be seen at the enterprising Norfolk and Suffolk Aviation Museum sited behind the 'Flixton Buck' public house, near Bungay.

Norfolk is the home for one Spitfire, suspended on a pedestal outside Station Headquarters, Coltishall. This is Mk 16 *SL542* whose active career began with 595 (AA Co-op) Squadron in August 1945. There it served for three years before passing to 695 Squadron in the summer of 1948. When anti-aircraft co-operation flying was placed in civilian hands *SL542* moved into No 1 CAACU, Hornchurch, where it was used until June 1951 before being placed into storage at 29 MU High Ercall. Following overhaul it was re-issued, joining No 2 CAACU at Little Snoring, Norfolk, in March 1954. A year later it came on to the strength of Station Flight, Duxford. An accident on 31 January 1957 caused its grounding after which it took on guard duty first at Horsham St Faith and then at Coltishall where its image is tarnished by an awful colour scheme. Please rescue it, someone!

East Anglia saw the Spitfire enter service, and indeed operate throughout the war, but Spitfires, although a daily wartime sight, were very much outnumbered by other types. It was the south and south-east of England that were the true Spitfire regions. One might reasonably expect each museum thereabouts to contain a Spitfire. What can one see of them there? Apart from one of the Battle of Britain film replicas in the Hawkinge Aeronautical Trust Museum at the former RAF station, and interesting assorted items of Battle of Britain memorabilia, there is sadly only one of the thousands of Spitfires that frequented those skies still left to view. Surrounded by a variety of associated items, it is another Mk 16, *TB752*, maintained by the Medway Branch, Royal Aeronautical Society, who were responsible for its superb restoration and its positioning in the Spitfire Memorial Building at Manston, an RAF station repeatedly bombed and strafed during the Battle of Britain. This Spitfire is of particular interest in that it was one of the limited number of Mk 16s not built with a 360° teardrop canopy. Initially with 66 Squadron at Fairwood Common, *TB752* moved to Holland then participated in daylight tactical bomber escort duties. Following a wheels-up landing on 25 March 1945 it was repaired, then went to 403 (Canadian) Squadron. On 19 April when being flown by Squadron Leader H. P. M. Zary, a Bf 109 was destroyed by its guns and four days later another enemy aircraft was downed. A third kill came on 1 May, a Fw 190 shot down by Flying Officer R. Young. *TB752* returned to England in August 1945 for storage at High Ercall and use as an exhibition aircraft. In 1951 it returned to flying, first with No 102 Flying Refresher School and then No 103 FRS, before going to High Ercall in August 1953. November 1953 saw it join No 5 CAACU, Llanbedr, before it retired a year later to 33 MU. It had a part in the film *Reach for the Sky* before it was grounded. September 1955 saw its arrival at Manston from whence it was removed in July 1978 to Rochester for restoration. On 15 September 1979, and in superb health, it took up residence at Manston, wearing the letters '*LZ:F*' in memory of its 66 Squadron days.

As in Kent, there is little in Surrey for the 'Spitfire spotter', although Leisure Sport's unusual collection at Thorpe Park, Chertsey is worth a call. Here may be seen a static replica of the Supermarine S.6 *S1595*, the 1931 Schneider Trophy winner. Leisure Sport maintains a collection of Schneider Trophy replicas, but its flying replica of the Supermarine S.5 *N220* (alias *G-BDFF*) sadly crashed on 23 September 1982. Sussex has recently seen exciting work undertaken to restore Spitfires to flying condition, but there are no museum exhibits in the county.

As for Hampshire's other Spitfires — apart from one at Southampton — those at Blackbushe will by now have probably all been taken to Bitteswell where Doug Arnold's Warbirds of Great Britain Collection is not open to the public, which is indeed a great shame for it holds many interesting aeroplanes. Among them, at the time of writing, are no less than seven Spitfires! Four of them are Mk XIVs, all ex-Indian Air Force, one is a Mk 16 *RW386*, one is a Mk IX ex-*NH238* and the rarest is a Mk 18 ex-*SM969*. The Mk XIVs are *MV293* now registered as *G-SPIT*, *SM832* now listed as *G-WWII*, *MV262* and *NH799*.

Wiltshire, whose Boscombe Down, High Post and Lyneham (through 33 MU) had such lengthy and intensive associations with Spitfires, has only one example likely to be seen, *LA226* due to return from Biggin Hill to Vickers' South Marston works.

Restoration work on Spitfires in the south-west is mentioned in the final chapter. A grounded example, a Mk 21, *LA198*, may be seen at RAF Locking and until 1985 RAF Brawdy, Dyfed, held *PS915*. The former was delivered to 1 Squadron in May 1945, entered storage in October 1946 and was issued to 602 Squadron in May 1947, serving until it was damaged in July 1949. Late September 1951 *LA198* joined No 3 CAACU, Exeter, which it vacated at the end of November 1953. After being grounded as *7118M*, *LA198* joined No 187 ATC Squadron at Worcester. In 1967 it was withdrawn and refurbished before taking up residence at Locking as '*JX:C*'. What the future holds for *PS915* is uncertain, but it looks very hopeful for the aircraft is currently being overhauled by British Aerospace at Warton with a view to a renewed flying career with the Battle of Britain Memorial Flight. *PS915*, a PR 19, was first used by 541 Squadron in the summer of 1945 and later that year was placed into Benson Station Pool as units there contracted. Next summer it joined the Photographic Reconnaissance Development Unit before being taken in October for overhaul and modification pending issue to No 2 Squadron in Germany in July 1948. Seriously damaged in April 1949 it was brought home for repair. Nearly two years later, in June 1954, it was placed in the THUM Flight at Woodvale from where it operated until June 1957. Then it moved to Biggin Hill for a possible part in the display flight. Instead, it was grounded and positioned first at West Malling and then at West Raynham before going to Leuchars. After being taken to Henlow for a part in *The Battle of Britain* film, *PS915* found its way to Brawdy. Its general condition is such that it will probably fly again.

At St Athan, South Glamorgan, Spitfire LF 9, *MK356*, is held as part of the RAF Museum's collection. In March 1944 the aircraft joined 443 (Canadian) Squadron at Digby and first operated, over France, on 14 April 1944. On 13 June 1944 it suffered damage during a wheels-up landing. The aircraft never flew again and became *5690M*. Following use at No 1 School of Technical Training, Halton, in 1951 it was moved to Hawkinge, residing there until 1961 when it was taken to Bicester for refurbishing. Subsequently it was displayed at RAF Locking and also had a ground role in the Battle of Britain film. After overhaul at Henlow in 1968 it was moved to St Athan where it resides bearing the letters '*2I:V*' of 443 Squadron.

Central England is the home of several non-flying Spitfires of which three are based at RAF Abingdon. Mk 22, *PK624*, shelters beneath trees near the camp entrance. It commenced squadron service with No 614 (County of Glamorgan) Squadron at Llandow in August 1948 and entered storage in October 1950. Vickers acquired the aircraft for an overseas sale which fell through. *PK624* returned to Service use and was placed first at Uxbridge then at Northolt in 1963. In 1968 it underwent major restoration and in July 1970 took up residence at Abingdon as '*RAU:T*' its current identity. Hidden is its true present serial, *8072M*.

Above *Spitfire LF 16 TB382 is one of the two examples frequently exhibited at air shows, and was at Finningley when this photograph was made.*

Below *In memory of thousands of Spitfires built there, Mk IX 6457M was long resident at Castle Bromwich.*

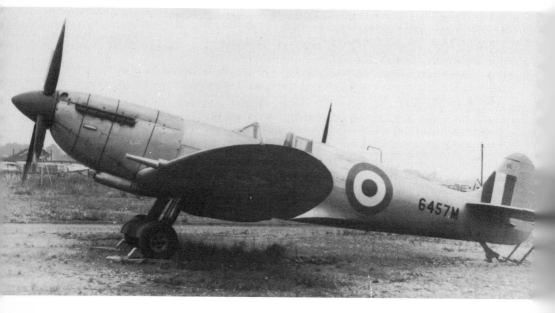

Abingdon's other two Spitfires are LF 16s and, being Exhibition Flight aircraft, are shown in various parts of the country. As '*LO:Z*', *TB382* came into use with 602 Squadron in the Coltishall Wing during February 1945 and flew over twenty fighter-bomber sorties. In July 1945 it entered storage from which it emerged in January 1949 to join the Fighter Command Communications Flight with whom it flew until seriously damaged on 31 May 1951. In December 1954, as *7244M*, it was placed at Thornaby, and later resided at Middleton-St-George. When that station closed it was exhibited at Ely RAF Hospital. Then it went to Henlow and was cleaned up, generally, for a ground part in the film *The Battle of Britain*. During 1969 it joined the Exhibition Flight.

Their other Mk 16 is *TE311*, which in October 1945 arrived at the Empire Central Flying School at Hullavington in whose hands it remained until February 1946. In 1951, following storage, it was placed in No 1689 Ferry Pilots Training Flight subsequently serving with the successor unit, the Ferry Training Unit, Benson based, until September 1953. There it briefly served No 2 CAACU Langham in 1954 before being stored at Lyneham. In August 1955 it became *7241M* and was moved to Tangmere. Retrieved in 1967 for *The Battle of Britain* film, and masquerading under a suitable disguise for a taxying part, it next returned in 1968 to its old home, Benson, for display. When Spitfire *SM411* was donated to the Museum of Aircraft and Astronautics in Krakow, Poland, in an exchange deal with the RAF Museum, *TE311* replaced that Spitfire in the Exhibition Flight.

At nearby Benson, long the home of RAF photo-reconnaissance, and from where during the war some of the most amazing of all operational sorties were mounted, a smart PR blue Spitfire Mk 19, *PM651*, sits just inside the entrance. Completed in 1945, the aircraft was kept in storage for nine years, until, in March 1954, it joined the THUM Flight at Woodvale. Its active days were abruptly terminated when on 14 April it crash landed on the station and was grounded. For a while it stood at Hucknall, then rested at Andover.

An exhibit with an uninspiring history is LF Mk 9, *ML427*, held by the Birmingham Museum of Science and Industry, Newhall Street, and which is open on weekdays and Sunday afternoons. *ML427*'s choice of markings is not exactly excellent, but the aircraft is well preserved. From May to late August 1945 it flew with the Fighter Leaders School, Millfield, Northumberland, then went into storage at 29 MU High Ercall. From late 1947 until summer 1954 it was used, as *6457M*, for instructional purposes at No 4 School of Technical Training, St Athan. August 1954 saw it placed at the gate of RAF Castle Bromwich, from where it entered the museum in 1958.

One might expect some worthwhile physical token of remembrance of the massive contribution that the Castle Bromwich factory made to Allied victory. Sadly that is not the case. The huge factory is very much intact and in the hands of British Leyland but the airfield has disappeared beneath a massive housing estate some of whose roads bear 'Spitfire' names. Apart from that, and a small 'notice', the Spitfire has all but vanished from Castle Bromwich — except in the memories of those who worked there with such dedication.

Not so at RAF Cosford. Responsible for training a vast army of technicians it is now the site of an extensive and most interesting collection of aircraft in its impressive Aerospace Museum (open daily 10:00 to 16:00 hours, but only Saturdays and Sundays in winter). Their Spitfire is *MT847*, an FR XIV built in 1945, delivered to 6 MU Brize Norton and held there until December 1945 when it was briefly used for trials at Boscombe Down which ended in February 1946. Following storage at 29 MU it was released in November 1950 to the Tac/Recon Training Flight of 226 OCU, Stradishall, and remained there until February 1952. Then it entered storage at 33 MU Lyneham, a unit which particularly specialized in handling Griffon Spitfires. In April *MT847* was taken to Warton, Lancashire, then was shuffled between training camps in that area. The Medical Training Establishment at Freckleton received it in 1955 and there it acquired the letters '*MT:E.*' Via other gate-guarding duties *MT847* arrived at Cosford in 1964.

Manchester's new Air & Space Museum in the preserved City Hall, Liverpool Road, received the smartly restored Mk Vb *BL614* on 7 December 1982. Delivered to the RAF in January 1942, it joined No 611 Squadron at Drem the following month and in June passed into the hands of 242 Squadron which exchanged its aircraft for those of 611 Squadron. Similarly, in August 1942 222 Squadron acquired it. A move to 64 Squadron at Hornchurch followed in April 1943, by which time the aircraft's wing tips had been clipped. In September 1943 *BL614* was transferred to 118 Squadron at Peterhead. In November No 3501 Servicing Unit Cranfield received it and *BL614* became *4354M*. After the war it could be seen first guarding the gate at Bridgnorth and later Credenhill. After restoration for the film, *The Battle of Britain*, it was, surprisingly, taken to Wattisham. As a replacement for Colerne's *P7350* which the Battle of Britain Memorial Flight acquired, *BL614* was sent along and was restored in 222 Squadron colours in which it is now exhibited.

The next nearest Spitfire is Mk 16 *TD248*, currently keeping an eye on those who enter the Officers' Mess at Sealand, Clwyd. Flown exclusively by anti-aircraft co-operation units, it was initially operated by 695 Squadron at Horsham St Faith and from September 1951 to 1954 by No 2 CAACU Little Snoring and Langham. After storage at 9 MU Cosford, it was issued to No 610 (County of Chester) Squadron, Hooton Park, where it acquired the letters 'DW:A'. After the RAuxAF disbanded in 1957 *TD248* was passed, as *7246M*, to No 1366 ATC Squadron.

Near to the Police Station in Bethesda Road, Hanley, Stoke-on-Trent, is the R. J. Mitchell Memorial containing a collection of items in his memory and relating to Supermarine. Opening hours are 09:00 to 13:00 and 13:30 to 17:30 (16:30 on Fridays), but the museum is closed on Thursdays and Sundays. Its prime exhibit is Spitfire 16, *RW388*, which in August 1945 joined No 667 Squadron at Gosport for anti-aircraft support work which it carried out until the end of that year. After storage and servicing, *RW388* joined No 5 Squadron at Chivenor. Then it was transferred to the Fighter Control and Reporting School at Middle Wallop for a brief active period before being grounded. Despatched some months later to Colerne, as *6946M*, it graced the gates of Andover and Benson and was then

Spitfires began guarding the gates of RAF stations in 1946. BM597/5713M, an LF Vb, is seen here during 1960 at the entrance to RAF Bridgnorth, Shropshire. Long resident at Church Fenton, marked 'PR:O', it is presently at Linton-on-Ouse.

stored, first at Kemble then St Athan from where it was taken for exhibition purposes, appearing as pseudo Mk V *'AB917'* before 71 MU took pity upon it, made it *RW388* once more, marked it as 'U4:U' (reckoned to be its original letters) and took it to its new home in February 1972.

Lincolnshire possesses but one Spitfire, Mk 22, *PK664*, pedestal mounted and residing at the entrance to Binbrook, home of the RAF's Lightning force. Not until May 1949 did this Spitfire come into active use, and became a familiar sight at Biggin Hill in the hands of No 615 (County of Surrey) Squadron with whom it operated until the end of 1950. Possible overseas sale did not materialize. Instead, *PK664* silver painted and unmarked despite its new identity as *7759M*, moved to RAF Waterbeach where it rested by the entrance. Some months after the station passed into Army hands, the RAF retrieved it and moved it to West Raynham then to Binbrook where it resides as 'V6:B' in a most unsuitable colour scheme.

There are two Spitfires in Yorkshire, LF Vb *BM597*, long resident at Church Fenton, and Leeming's Mk 16 *TE356*. The former is the more interesting since it operated with two Polish Squadrons, No 315 from May to September 1942 and then with 317 Squadron until February 1943. During that entire period it was Woodvale based. Servicing and storage followed, and not until almost the end of the war did it emerge to join 58 OTU, where it stayed until October 1945. When it was taken subsequently to No 4 School of Technical Training, St Athan, it became *5713M*. Later the aircraft kept an eye on those entering Hednesford, Bridgnorth, and Church Fenton where a kind person took pity upon it and decorated it as 'PR:O' of No 609 Squadron. In 1967 it was snatched for an unusual role in *The Battle of Britain* film, since it formed the basis from which the replica fibreglass Spitfires for the film were prepared. August 1968 saw it return to Henlow, then the next year it slipped back into its quiet corner at Church Fenton. When that station went on to Care & Maintenance *BM597* emigrated to Church Fenton's old friend, Linton-on-Ouse, where a smart *BM597* now resides.

Few Spitfires in retirement retained their original unit or squadron markings. An exception was Mk XVI TE356. Used as '8Q:Z' by 34 Squadron, it continued to wear these letters when with 2 CAACU at Little Snoring. They were still in place when (technically as 6709M) it went on parade at Bicester. Currently it resides at Leeming.

Leeming's *TE356* is supported by a pole arising from a stone circle, a curious state for a Spitfire! Yet another emigrant from the world of anti-aircraft co-operation, *TE356* served with 695 Squadron from July 1945, and was still on strength when in February 1949 the squadron was re-numbered No 34 Squadron. It later flew with No 2 CAACU at Little Snoring and Langham, until it was grounded on 1 September 1952, becoming *6709M* subsequent to which it rested at Bicester as a guardian. It awoke to the call of *The Battle of Britain* film in 1967 and played an active part during the filming at North Weald before retiring to the Central Flying School at Kemble where doubtless it envied the excitement of the Gnats of 'The Red Arrows'! The strain obviously being too much, it was taken away to CFS headquarters at Little Rissington, and then via Cranwell in 1976 to Leeming. Its future residence is very uncertain.

In Scotland there are three Spitfires, *RW393* at Turnhouse, *TB252* at Leuchars, Fife and *TE462* at East Fortune, Lothian. Mk 16 *RW393* was first active with No 203 Advanced Flying School, Chivenor from November 1947. Then in January 1948 it was moved to the Fighter Command Control and Reporting School, Middle Wallop. In 1950 *RW393* became the prestigious personal transport of the C-in-C Fighter Command, Air Marshal Sir William Elliot, and was serviced by 31 Squadron. October 1953 saw its posting to No 3 CAACU, Exeter, from where it retired to 45 MU Kinloss in July 1954. After issue to No 603 Squadron, RAuxAF as *7293M*, it was placed on display at Turnhouse in 1957 where, as '*XT:A*', it still resides in surprisingly smart appearance.

TB252 is one of those Spitfire 16s which did not have a teardrop canopy. It was also one of the relatively few Mk 16s to see operational service in 1945, after joining 329 (Free French) Squadron, the 'les Cicoques', at Turnhouse, early in March. Its active moments were halted when, within a few days, it needed field repairs. Then it joined No 341 (Free French) Squadron. In November 1945 *TB252* joined No 135 Wing and in January was switched to 350 (Belgian) Squadron at Fassberg with whom it served until October 1946. In mid-1947 it joined 61 OTU at Keevil and was still there when the unit became 203 Advanced Flying School. In January 1949 *TB252* was placed at Old Sarum. As *7257M* the aircraft moved to Odiham in September 1955 and, in 1959 went to Acklington where it acquired the letters '*RR:M*'. July 1969 saw its movement to Boulmer, Northumberland and in December it made its way to Leuchars where it currently resides as '*GW:H*', pretending to be, curiously, with 340 (Free French) Squadron.

Scotland's other Spitfire, another Mk 16, is *TE462* held by the Royal Scottish Museum's Museum of Flight, an out-station at East Fortune, Lothian and open to viewing only during summer months. *TE462* had a very limited flying career, first with Finningley's Station Flight between October 1950 and April 1951 and then with No 101 Flying Refresher School where it was in use until at least late 1953. Then, at High Ercall, it became *7243M* and in August 1955 was placed at Ouston's Main Gate. When in 1970 that station's active life was halted, *TE462* was despatched to Kemble. After refurbishing at Bicester, the Spitfire was moved to East Fortune in February 1971.

Ulster's only Spitfire is yet another Mk 16, *TE184*, sited in the Ulster Folk and Transport Museum, Holywood, Co Down, and for some time in storage. Stored

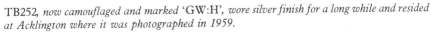

*TB252, now camouflaged and marked '*GW:H*', wore silver finish for a long while and resided at Acklington where it was photographed in 1959.*

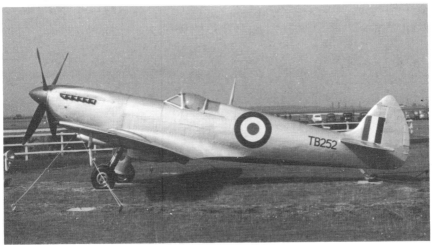

until September 1948, it then joined 203 Advanced Flying School at Chivenor from which an element (including *TE184*) was hived off to join 226 Operational Conversion Unit with whom this Spitfire served until February 1950. Then it joined the Training Flight of No 607 Squadron, RAuxAF, at Ouston before going into storage at 33 MU Lyneham in June. In November 1950 *TE184* resumed an active career by joining the Central Gunnery School at Leconfield. An accident on 30 January 1951 led to it being grounded and becoming *6850M* at No 64 Reserve Centre, Long Benton, Newcastle. In 1952 No 1855 ATC Squadron, Royton, Lancashire, received the aircraft, then in 1967 it was moved to Finningley's collection and partly refurbished. Via Kemble and Aldergrove, it made its way to the Irish museum, as '*LA:A*', the markings of 607 (County of Durham) Squadron.

In Britain there appear to be 39 complete grounded or 'museum' Spitfires, although the possibility always remains, just, that from a secret Aladdin's cave several more may one day emerge. Travel from our shores and there are more Spitfires to be seen, but probably no more than thirty.

In Paris, the Musée de l'Air holds Mk 9 *BS464* and also a Mk 16 which 66 Squadron once operated and which is painted in 340 Squadron's colours.

The Brussels Musée de l'Armée et d'Histoire Militaire has Mk 9 *MJ783*, alias *SM15*, used by the Belgian Air Force between 1948 and 1951, and is restoring Mk 14 *MV246*. At Soesterberg, Netherlands, resides Mk 9 *MJ143*, alias *H-1*, RNethAF, which at one time was 3W:I of the Netherlands' 322 Squadron. Overloon open air Museum has PR 11 *PL965*, and Schiphol's Museum holds Mk 9 *MJ271* '*H-53*'. Copenhagen's Royal Danish Arsenal Museum contains Mk 9 *NH417*, alias *41–401*. Another such, *MH350* and ex-349 and 331 Squadrons, is in Norway along with a PR 11 *PL979* marked '*ZB:A*' and kept at Gardemoen. *MJ755*, yet another Mk 9, prefers the warmth of Athens.

Venture to Czechoslovakia and Prague Military Museum's Mk 16 *TE565*, once of the Czech Fighter Wing, will doubtless be delighted at the whiff of freedom you bring! Poland holds at least two Spitfires, one (*SM411*) residing at Krakow. PR Mk 19 *PM627* is in Sweden's Linkoping Museum and Mk 9 *MK805/MM4084* in the Italian Air Force Vigna de Valle Museum.

In Mingaladon an ex-Burmese Air Force Mk 9, *UB431*, survives and the Royal Thai Air Force Museum has a Spitfire FR 14. Of two Spitfire VIIIs, *A58-671/ex-MV154* and *A58-758/ex-MV239* long resident at Bankstown, in Australia, *MV154* has now received a new lease of life in Britain, leaving Spitfire II *P7973* '*R-H*', which reached Australia in July 1945, as a monument in the National War Museum, Canberra. In New Zealand, Auckland War Museum exhibits Spitfire 16 *TE456*, which in its RAF days was seen at 3 and 4 CAACUs. The Canterbury Brevet Club holds *TE288*, a Mk 16 which served at 61 OTU; with 501 Squadron, Filton; No 102 Flying Refresher School at North Luffenham; and as a display aircraft prior to being taken to New Zealand in 1963.

Held by the Canadian National Aeronautical Collection, Rockcliffe Air Station, Ontario, are three Spitfires including a most unusual Mk IIb *P8332* at one time with 222 Squadron, and Mk 9 *NH188* which served with 308 (Polish) and 416 (Canadian) Squadrons before post-war service in the Netherlands and Belgium

Beautiful, SL721 looked, as Air-Marshal James Robb taxied the blue Spitfire to greet our station commander. Sadly, it is now abroad.

where, after serving as *SM39*, it wore the civil identity *OO-ARC*. It was sold to Canada as *CF-NUS*, and later donated to the Aeronautical Collection. The third machine is Spitfire 16 *TE214* which carries the letters '*DN:T*' identifying it as a 416 Squadron machine. Also in Canada is a Spitfire Vb, once *7555M*, which stood by the gates of both Bridgnorth and Dishforth.

Across the border a Spitfire 1 *P9306* can be seen in the Museum of Science and Industry, Chicago. This is a particularly distinguished aircraft being credited with five enemy aircraft during its service with 74 Squadron. The late Air Chief Marshal Sir James Robb's 'personal' Spitfire, one time bright blue *SL721* which carried his initials '*JMR*' has also gone to the USA, via Lord Montague's Beaulieu Motor Museum. Probably the most photographed and best known of the American Spitfires must be the Confederate Air Force's Mk 9 which carries the letters '*D:B*' in memory of Douglas Bader. This was previously *G-ASSD*. For some time the 'CAF' also operated a Mk 14, *N2OE* (ex-*CF-GMZ* and *TZ138*). Other Spitfires which have made their way to the USA have included LF Mk IXs *MK297* (*N1882*) ex-*H55* of the RNethAF, *MK923* (ex-*H-61* and latterly *NX521R*) and *NH238* (ex-*H-60*) which became *N238V*.

These, then, are some of the many Spitfires which it is generally possible to see. Many remain in military hands and permission may have to be sought if they are to be viewed, especially by any resident outside of the United Kingdom.

Of course, you will probably prefer to see — and hear — a Spitfire roaring by! Your choice then will be more limited for the cost of keeping a Spitfire flying is high, which means that only on special occasions will it be possible to see a Spitfire in flight. Such exotic creatures are naturally expensive beings requiring very expert handling. Perhaps you would like to own one?

Chapter 11
Come see my Spitfire FLY!

Do you still want your very own Spitfire? Well, if you achieve that you will join a very select band of enthusiasts, and need a very healthy bank balance. To find out whether such a move was possible I decided to visit Robert Brooks of Christies. He it is who auctions Spitfires, so surely he would know the position — and the problems of acquiring one.

Christies' summer auctions at Duxford are the first in Britain at which historic and aged aircraft have been sold. Among them have been Spitfires, the firm having handled their first Spitfire sale in 1968. Since then five more Spitfire sales have been negotiated, of which the best known was probably that involving the Mk 9 *MH434*.

Before any sale can come about expert valuation is necessary. How much, then, is likely to be needed for the purchase of a Spitfire? For a flying example in fine condition a sum of perhaps £350,000 will need to change hands. That daunting figure does not, of course, include spares, which would prove to be an expensive addition. Even so, the market is strong and there are many people, groups and organizations interested nowadays in acquiring such prestigious and fascinating symbols.

Perhaps surprisingly, most interest seems to be in obtaining a Spitfire Mk V, although if a famed Mk1 was to come forward for purchase doubtless the number wishing to purchase would be high. The second most popular acquisition is probably a Mk XIV. In either case, the running expenses during flying would be about £1,000 an hour, although many factors can influence such a figure. Currently, Spitfires in private hands may expect to fly for about thirty to forty hours a year. Some of that enormous expense can be retrieved by offering the aircraft to appear at air displays or other public events. But the cost of attending, even if a free fuel load is obtained in the process, could well exceed any remuneration. Grand though it must be to take one's own Spitfire to a party, and to reap a handsome reward in knowing that something beautiful is being shared and bringing much pleasure, the fact remains that it is a costly experience.

During my conversation with Robert Brooks he suggested that while some Spitfires were rebuilt around a very battered or perhaps limited collection of initial parts, there might well be interest in the field of replicas. If a full scale plastic Spitfire can be built, surely a flying replica is a distinct possibility. At the

Another beautifully cared for example, and a splendid performer, is the Mk 9 MH434 often flown by the one-time Red Arrows' leader, Ray Hanna.

same time the recovery of Spitfire parts from distant, unlikely places is not going to stop, so we may even see the restoration of a Spitfire around parts of one flown by a famous ace. Such a scenario is not all that far fetched.

One of the biggest problems to face once one has acquired a Spitfire lies in keeping its engine in excellent health. Since so many Merlins were built the problem is not as difficult as it might at first seem — particularly if one of the more plentiful American-built Packard Merlins or a Mk 25 is involved. Items from scrapped Merlins or resulting from part exchanges have often proven vital in keeping engines in good state. Thus, quite a number of the Spitfires still flying are powered by what amount to hybrid powerplants, or have engines differing from original installations. Merlin 32s from Boulton Paul Balliol trainers have, for instance, been most useful. Overhauls of Merlins, again a costly venture, have been undertaken of late in such far parted places as Jersey in the Channel Islands (where Jersey Aviation has a store of spares) and by Jack Hovey in California, USA, who has specialized in Packard Merlins. But if engines are a problem, what better than to enquire of Rolls-Royce what powerplant problems have to be faced? That I discussed with Mr M. H. Evans in whose care the company has placed its Griffon-engined Spitfire 14 *G-ALGT*.

It was very clear from what he had to tell me that to maintain a Spitfire is now a demanding task, particularly if a Certificate of Airworthiness is to be annually renewed. To achieve that coveted document the aircraft needs stringent checks, and investigations to a schedule could well require that some parts be X-rayed to ensure all was well. In particular the undercarriage needs close scrutiny, cleaning and re-greasing. In 1985, *G-ALGT* needed a re-make of its flap bearings, attention to its radiator, new perspex in the cockpit canopy and problems with the engine temperature gauge had to be cleared. Much of that work required the manufacture of items no longer available, and the adaptation of others — bearing in mind modern safety needs.

After every 2,000 running hours the engine of the Rolls-Royce Spitfire undergoes a complete overhaul. Particularly prone to wear are the valve springs and cylinder liners. During an engine re-work a cylinder block change becomes essential, and the problems involved are then accentuated by the need for specialized, almost 'exotic' tools, with which to rebuild the engine. The special washers needed within parts of the engine must fit tightly — and that is a far from easy task to achieve. Without the particular tools needed for dismantling the engine and rebuilding the block, such tasks are extremely difficult. Such activities need co-operative efforts, so it is not surprising that there is a ready exchange of parts and expertise among Spitfire owners. During 1985 Rolls-Royce was able to help other Spitfire owners with the loan of engine starters. The Griffon position is aided to some degree by the RAF's continued use of the Avro Shackleton AEW2 which means that Griffon spares have been maintained over a very long period.

Pioneer civilian Spitfire owner was a businessman, M. L. Bramson, who shortly after the war was first to purchase one for his personal and company use. He acquired an extremely rare specimen, a Spitfire IIb *P8727*, constructor's number 'CBAF 960'. After serving with the Central Gunnery School it had joined No 276 Air/Sea Rescue Squadron. Bramson obtained it after the aircraft was struck off RAF charge on 30 April 1945. In the course of a complete rebuild, Marshall of Cambridge installed a Merlin 45, the aircraft was finished in black and decorated in yellow and the name 'Josephine' was applied before it received a C of A on 22 October 1946. Its base was Elstree, but an early demise came on 15 April 1947 when *G-AHZI* was destroyed when taking off from Kastrup, Copenhagen.

With a post-war surfeit of Spitfires, Vickers was naturally interested in the aircraft's sales potential. Since it had sold its wares to the government, it would need to re-purchase Spitfires to be able to export them. One possible sale was to Egypt, and to enable its pilots to train to fly Spitfires Vickers bought a Mk VIII, *MT818*, and fitted a raised cockpit aft of the normal one devising a Spitfire Trainer which became *G-AIDN*. That it has survived to this day is certainly surprising. When landing at Coventry in 1978 it suffered an undercarriage failure and at the time of writing is being rebuilt in the USA where it arrived in March 1983. In 1985 it took on the identity of *MT818*, was painted in RAF colours and was marked 'G:M,' the initials of its owner Mr G. F. Miller.

Vickers also acquired a Mk IX and converted that into a Trainer. Registered *G-ALJM* In July 1949, the aircraft was delivered to Egypt in March 1950. A second Mk VIII Trainer, *G-AKBD* had been acquired by Vickers on 14 July 1947 but was not proceeded with and the conversion was cancelled in May 1948. Another Vickers-modified Mk IX Trainer, *MJ627*, was sold to the Irish Air Corps and became '158'. Brought back to Biggin Hill and then taken to Elstree, this one was dismembered at the end of 1964. It main components were removed

At Duxford for the film The Battle of Britain, *was this two-seater* G-AIDN — *very useful for filming from* — *and accompanied by a genuine RAF man!*

to Stockbridge three years later from where its present owners, M. S and P. K. Bayliss, transported it to Warwickshire in 1978 with the intention of having it flying again. *G-AIDN*, the Mk 8 Trainer, may well be flying in 1986.

But what of Spitfires already flying in 1986, and likely to roar by recalling the great Spitfire days? Unquestionably, one of the most impressive, and one which looks as it did in 1944 when twice I saw it in its hey-day, is the LF 9 *MH434*. In August 1943 its operational life began at Hornchurch with 222 Squadron in whose hands three enemy fighters fell to its guns. When the Squadron moved out for rest late that year 350 (Belgian) Squadron replaced No 222, and briefly operated its aircraft. No 222 retrieved *MH434* but it was soon away again, transferred to 349 (Belgian) Squadron and at the end of the war it was put into storage, first at Cosford then Wroughton. Its battle days were however, far from over, for in May 1947 it joined the Royal Netherlands Air Force, became *H-105* and in October 1947 joined 322 Squadron in Java and flew strike missions during the Dutch attempt to keep their East Indies territory. Such activity was halted when on 7 May 1949 the aircraft, by now identified as *H-68*, belly landed at Kalibenteng.

MH434 has certainly been a lucky 'survivor' for it was shipped back to the Netherlands where Fokker, identifying it as *B-13*, overhauled it prior to sale in October 1953 to the Belgian Air Force who re-named it 'SM 41'. During March 1956 it was sold to COGEA and as *OO-ARA* served as a target tug from its Ostend home. In 1963 the aircraft was purchased by Mr T. Davies, taken to Elstree for overhaul and resumed flying as *G-ASJV*, for in those days the decoration of British civil aircraft in military garb was highly unauthorized!

Late in 1967 *G-ASJV* joined the ever growing number of 'Spitfires' being assembled for *The Battle of Britain* film, after which Adrian Swire purchased it

and marked it appropriately *'AC:S'. MH434* was the Spitfire which in April 1983 hit the headlines by being sold in a Christies' Duxford auction for £260,000 to Ray Hanna's group (Nalfire Aviation) which has operated it from Duxford.

Another of the frequently flown Spitfires is *G-AIST*, owned by the Honourable Patrick Lindsay, an international director of Christies, and based at Booker. Wearing late wartime camouflage, and lettered *'QG:A'* as used by 53 Operational Training Unit, this is Spitfire Mk la, *AR213* a Westland-built aircraft, delivered in July 1941 and used first by 57 OTU. In February 1943 it was transfered to 53 OTU which used it until August 1944 when it was placed in the Aircraft Storage Unit at Little Rissington. The late Air Commodore Allen Wheeler purchased it in March 1947 and subsequently it entered long term storage at Old Warden. Good protection enabled it to be refurbished for a flying part in *The Battle of Britain* film, after which it found a home at Booker. There Allen Wheeler sold it to the present owner, who maintains it in superb condition.

Although the Shuttleworth Collection had lost *AR213* its place was taken by a Spitfire Vc, *AR501*, often to be seen flying at Old Warden, and sometimes found sheltering at Duxford. Also from the Westland line, this is a clipped-wing Mk Vb whose squadron career began in July 1942 when it joined No 310 (Czech) Squadron at Exeter. Its identity letters *'NN:D'* date from that period, and were by lucky chance obtained from one of its wartime pilots who now lives near Duxford. Between March 1943 and August 1943 the aircraft underwent repair, overhaul and storage before joining Church Stanton Station Flight. October 1943 saw it enter 312 Squadron at Ibsley and when that Squadron re-equipped with Mk IXs in February 1944, *AR501* went to the newly forming 442 Squadron, RCAF, at Digby where it briefly served in a training capacity before joining No 2 Tactical Exercise Unit (previously called 2 Combat Training Wing and before that 58 OTU) at Grangemouth. Within a few weeks No 1 TEU was using it and in July 1944 it joined 61 OTU with whom it served until early September. Repairs and servicing were followed by four months' summer duty at the Central Gunnery School from which it entered storage at 29 MU High Ercall in late August 1945.

In March 1946 Loughborough College of Engineering acquired *AR501* and not until 1961 did it leave, for the Shuttleworth Collection. Still in good condition, it was rapidly restored to flying state as *G-AWII* for *The Battle of Britain* film. Then it lodged briefly at RAE Bedford before a two-year complete rebuild was undertaken at Duxford by a group of skilled, dedicated enthusiasts whose joy was measureless when the late, sadly missed Neil Williams took it aloft for the first time in June 1975. A superb Spitfire, for sure.

Top left AR213 *marked 'QG:A' was grounded for a long time before being restored and flown during* The Battle of Britain *filming. Presently it is owned by the Hon Patrick Lindsay who keeps it at Booker.*

Centre left *One of the most beautifully restored of all Spitfires, LF Vb AR501 of* The Shuttleworth Collection *wearing the markings of the Czech 310 Squadron.*

Left *Spitfire T 9s of the Irish Air Corps.*

The prospects of seeing several more Mk 9s flying are good. One which became airborne again in 1985 was a two-seater, with its second cockpit covered by a hood similar to the front one which, maybe, points to a new line. This example, *ML407* (alias *G-LFIX*), has been finished as '*OU:V*' of 485 (New Zealand) Squadron with which it operated between May and October 1944 and again briefly in December, before passing among Nos 308 (Polish), 332 (Norwegian), 341 (Free French), 349 (Belgian) and again 485 Squadron before being returned to Britain from 2 TAF in September 1945. Stored at 29 MU until July 1950, *ML407* was subsequently sold to Vickers. There it was converted into a T.Mk 9 for the Irish Air Corps which received it, as '*162*', in June 1951 and placed it in A Flight, Fighter Squadron at Baldonnel and operated it from there until 1960. During the ensuing eight years it served as an instructional aircraft.

Purchased and then brought to England, it was stored at Cricklewood, before joining the Strathallan Collection from which in August 1979 the present owner, E. N. Grice obtained it for a rebuild at St Merryn. In September 1985, it starred in the BBC film of the Finningley Display.

A close relative, yet one with a totally different life story, is *ML417*, frequently flown from Duxford in recent months. Unusual on account of its broad chord, tall rudder, it wears the identity of No 443 Squadron RCAF, with which it operated for much of the period between late June to mid-October 1944. Then it served with 401 Squadron RCAF, and subsequently was also flown by 401, 411, 412 and again 443 Canadian Squadrons before arriving at 29 MU in August 1945. From there in late 1946 it was sold to Vickers who converted it into a trainer for the

An unexpected newcomer to the flying scene has been this LF Mk 9e, ML417. Discovered by an American Senator near New Delhi, India, it was shipped to the USA for restoration. Collector of veteran aeroplanes, Stephen Grey, then bought it from him for his flying collection. It has spent much time at Duxford.

Indian Air Force which knew it as *HS543*. In the late 1970s it was acquired by an American who sold it to Stephen Grey. He had it shipped to Britain and Personal Plane Services at Booker restored it to superb health as *G-BJSG*/alias *ML417* and marked as '*21:T*'. Such is its excellent condition that Stephen Grey flies this, like other aircraft in his exciting fleet of 'warbirds', between Britain and his home in Switzerland. Do not be surprised if you should have a fleeting glimpse of *ML417* at Sion, resting by the main railway line between Geneva and Brig. This Spitfire, incidentally, is a Mk 9 with a Packard Merlin 266 although it has not become a true 16 for it lacks other necessary modifications. It isn't a true Mk 9 either!

Which other Mk 9s are likely to be regularly flying remains to be seen. *G-AVAV* (ex-*MJ772*) which became two-seater '*159*' of the Irish Air Corps is a possibility for recovery. It returned to Britain in 1967, registered as owned by N. A. Samuelson, Elstree, for use in *The Battle of Britain* film after which it passed via Shoreham to the Strathallan Collection. Samuelson, incidentally, also purchased the Irish Air Corps '*163*' for the same purpose. This, which started life as *TE308*, became *G-AWBD* and following the film was sold to Canada as *CF-RAF*.

Incidentally, two other 9s which also crossed the Atlantic were *G-ASSD* and *G-AVDJ*. The former *MK297* (CBAF No *1514*), sold to the Dutch on 12 February 1948, was used in Java as *H-55* of 322 Squadron, RNethAF and later by the Belgian Air Force as *SM 43* before becoming *OO-ARB* to serve as a target tug. In June 1966 it arrived at Cambridge for restoration which was never completed. Its owner, Mr J. Crewdson, was killed in a helicopter tragedy over the Wash and in May 1969 the aircraft was sold and became *N1882* of the Confederate Air Force which has also since disposed of it. *MH415* was previously *H-108*, then *H-65* of the RNethAF. Within a few days of joining 322 Squadron in Java it crash landed and was returned to Fokker for repair. Subsequently it was sold to Belgium and became *SM 40* of the Belgian Air Force and later *OO-ARD*. Brought to Britain for *The Battle of Britain* film, it was registered *G-AVDJ* prior to its sale in November 1968 to Conny Edwards at Big Spring, USA, as *N415H*.

Five more Mk 9s in Britain are in various stages of being restored for flying. *PV202* which served the Irish Air Corps as '*161*' and is now registered as *G-TRIX* is in the keeping of a Saffron Walden engineer. Mr Douglas Arnold, who has moved his base from Blackbushe to Bitteswell, has Mk 9 *NH238*. Delivered to the RNethAF in October 1947, it became *H103* then *H60* during its Indonesian service. Fokker overhauled it and repainted it as *B8*. Sold then to the Belgian Air Force, it became *SM 36* before COGEA at Ostend acquired it, as *OO-ARE*. Then it was sold to the USA where it became *N238V* of the Confederate Air Force which had it painted as *EN398* and marked '*JE:J*' to represent a Spitfire flown by 'Johnnie' Johnson. Subsequently it joined 'Yesterday's Air Force' at Chino, California before re-crossing the Atlantic to be restored as *NH238* alias *G-MKIX*. In Britain it has hugged the shade.

One can only imagine the fascinating career of Mk 9 *G-BLCK*, ex-*TE566*, being rebuilt by Aero Vintage Ltd of St Leonard's. After wartime service with No 312 (Czech) Squadron it was stored before joining the Czech Air Force. Then it became '*32*' of the Israeli Defence Force. Somewhat battered, yet fairly intact, it

A rare sight indeed, the Spitfire HF VIII MV154 resting in 1959 in its old home, Sydney Technical College. Now it is in England, owned by Robs Lamplough.

was rescued from an Israeli kibbutz in 1976 and later brought home. Its owner, Robs Lamplough, then sold it to the present owner, Guy Black.

A sun-scorched companion being restored by the same concern is *G-BLAS*, a Mk 9 (ex-*MJ730*), which after service in the Mediterranean Theatre was disposed of to the Italian Air Force who knew it as *MM4094*. Next, it became '*66*' of the Israel Defence Force. This one, too, was rescued, albeit in a very unhealthy state. Guy Black purchased it from Robs Lamplough and much effort has gone into restoring it for flying displays in 1986.

Also brought to Britain from a hot clime is a now-rare Mk 8, *MV154*. Shipped to Australia in late 1944, it became *A58-671* of the Royal Australian Air Force in whose hands it remained until 1949. In that year *A58-671* was sold to Sydney Technical College, from whom it passed to Syd Marshall of Bankstown. He sold it to Robs Lamplough who managed to ship it to Britain by declaring it to be not a banned export but a load of scrap metal. At the end of 1979 it reached Duxford and then was taken to Specialized Mouldings Ltd of Huntingdon, builders of Duxford's plastic Spitfire replica. It has been restored to flying condition under the identity *MV154/G-BKMI* and is with the Fighter Wing Display Team.

There are presently four Mk 16s being restored to flying condition and a reasonable assumption is that they will be joined by others discharged from gate guarding activities at RAF camps. By offering a replica Sopwith Pup to the RAF Museum, Doug Arnold's Warbirds of Great Britain based at Bitteswell acquired Spitfire LF 16 *RW386* from Halton, and it is now registered *G-BXVI*. Between March 1947 and early 1949 this Spitfire served with 604 (County of Middlesex) Squadron at Hendon, initially as '*RAK:A*' and later '*NG:D*' when the RAuxAF was given a front line role. Technical Training Command flew it from Debden, as '*S:C*' of the College there. Upon the unit's demise *RW386* was taken to 58 MU where it became *6944M*. A spell at Honington's gate followed before *RW386* found its way in 1957 to No 1 School of Technical Training Halton where it was redecorated as '*RAK:A*' of 604 Squadron. It would be good to see a Mk 16 flying once more, and the presence of another Mk 16 *TE392* taken from the gate of Credenhill in 1985 for likely restoration makes this even more probable.

Another Spitfire LF 16 is *TB863* alias *G-CDAN* being rebuilt at Booker. Life has dealt very harshly with the machine whose film career ended by it being dumped in a ditch and much overgrown before rescue came. That was most unjustified for an aircraft which, as '*FU:P*' of 453 Squadron and Matlaske based, began fighter-bomber operations on 24 March 1945, flying three sorties over the Netherlands on that day. After another four sorties the squadron moved, taking '*P*-Peter' to Lympne and on 13 April, from an advanced base, *TB863* helped to escort Lancasters raiding Swinemunde. Further such operations involved covering a Lancaster raid upon Heligoland and the 24 April raid upon Wangeroog. Two days later the aircraft supported the disembarkation of British troops in Guernsey and Jersey. After the war came service with anti-aircraft co-operation squadrons, *TB863* being with 691 Squadron when that was renumbered 17 Squadron at Chivenor in February 1949. In March 1951 it was transferred to No 3 CAACU, Exeter, where it was damaged beyond repair the following summer. Metro-Goldwin-Mayer bought it for possible use in the film *Reach for the Sky*, after which the aircraft deteriorated during time at Pinewood Studios. Parts were cannibalized for use in *The Battle of Britain* film, after which it found its way to Southend where its owner, Mr Francis, kept it in his garden. It was found languishing in very sorrowful state in a hangar at Duxford before heading for Southam, Warwickshire, where Mr Francis had moved. Restoration to flying condition has been undertaken by Personal Plane Services of Booker and its present owner is Stephen Grey.

What is surprising is the number of Mk XIV, Griffon-engined Spitfires that are now flying, some after long periods of ill health. Costly to run on account of their very powerful, thirsty engines, they have one advantage in that powerplant spares are still in good supply in Britain. Unquestionably one of the most beautiful of all Spitfires flying is Classic Air Displays' bright red and white trimmed FR 14 *NH904* flying as *G-FIRE*. Although it joined 414 Squadron RCAF in April 1944, its operational career was brief, for almost immediately it was involved in a wheels-up landing. After the war it joined 610 Squadron at Hooton Park following which the Belgian Air Force used it as *SG 108* at its Coxyde based Fighter School. After being sold off it sadly watched the passers-by from the roof of a scrap yard near Ostend until, in 1966, a car dealer took pity on it, handed over £250 and took the aircraft to Cheshire. By amalgamating the parts with those of another Mk 14, *RM694*, he was able to produce a respectable looking Spitfire 14 for his garage forecourt. It fell into the net of the film makers in 1967 as they scoured the land for Spitfires irrespective of their suitability. Its film days were spent at Henlow where Sir William Roberts came to its rescue. Eventually he placed it at Strathallan, but early in 1979 he sold it to Spencer Flack who carried it off south for restoration. In March 1981 it again took to the air from Elstree, flown by Ray Hanna of 'Red Arrows' fame, and it is now a frequent sight at air displays.

Strange are the sitings of many an historic aeroplane, but none more so, surely than that of Spitfire 14 *MV370* alias *G-FXIV* which in 1983 was bought in partly restored state by Paul Raymond. After completion it was painted as '*VL:A*' and then placed in the London War Museum, actually the old Whitehall Theatre converted for a purpose which displeased Ken Livingstone's GLC. As a result the museum was closed and the Spitfire was acquired by Robs Lamplough for restoration to flying at a suitable time. Most of its Service life had been spent in India and after the war it served in the Indian Air Force as *T44*. This was one of a number of Spitfires brought back from India in 1978 by the then well-known Haydon-Baillie whose exotic fleet of T-33 jets, among other types, was Duxford based. After his death the Spitfire was acquired by Keith Wickenden and colleagues who placed it in the 1983 Christies' auction, after which Paul Raymond was attracted to it.

Another Mk 14 likely to fly again is *SM832*, registered for the purpose as *G-WWII*. Its Service career was in India and in 1947 it was sold to the Indian Air Force, from whom it was acquired by Douglas Arnold for the Warbirds Collection at Bitteswell. Compared with many, this Spitfire was in quite good condition when it came home. Another Mk 14 with a similar history is *MV293* which reached India in the autumn of 1945 and was sold to the Indian Air Force in late 1947. Shipped back to Britain after purchase by Mr Arnold, the aircraft was registered *G-SPIT* and the intention is also to fly this one.

A smart looking Mk 14 no longer flying in Britain is *NH749/G-MXIV*. Despatched to India in July 1945, it was sold to the Indian Air Force in late 1947. Ten years later it was one of seven Spitfires bought by Ormond Haydon-Baillie and returned to Britain. There it was sold to Keith Wickenden who had it restored in SEAC markings. It flew again in 1983 and then, following Keith Wickenden's death was sold to a Los Angeles businessman, David Price, who in July 1984 based his beautifully-restored Spitfire at Chino, Southern California. It flies now as *H749* and holds the American identity *NX749DP*.

A rarity in the hands of Douglas Arnold is a Mk 18, ex-*SM969*, registered as *G-BRAF* and yet another fugitive from the Indian Air Force which knew it as *HS877*. It went to India in early 1946 but may have been removed to the Middle East prior to joining the Indian Air Force. 'Warbirds' acquired it in 1978 and as the ultimate Spitfire prior to the 20 series, this is an aircraft that would be well worth having flying again.

Its unique quality is shared by the all-blue Spitfire PR XI *PL983*, owned by Roland Fraissinet, a Frenchman who often has his splendid possession in his homeland, but sometimes keeps it at Castle Donington. For many years it rested in the open at Old Warden. Its RAF service began late 1944 when it found its way to that Mecca of photo-reconnaissance, RAF Benson. In January 1944 it joined No 4 Squadron, switching to No 2 Squadron in September of that year. January 1946 saw it enter storage, before in July 1947 Vickers acquired it and, after overhaul, placed it in January 1948 in the hands of the United States Air Attaché registered as *N74138*. Well-known pilot Lettice Curtis flew the aircraft and was piloting it when it hit the headlines by taking part in the 1948 Lympne Air Race.

Vickers retrieved *PL983* in 1950 and almost at once passed it to the Shuttleworth Collection at Old Warden. In August 1975 it was moved to Duxford, to be restored to flying condition. Financial constraints within the Collection led instead to its sale for £110,000 at Christies' 1983 Duxford auction. That sale resulted in it being moved to Trent Aero Engineering Ltd, of Stonebroom, Derbyshire, where it was restored for flying, as *G-PRIX*. An attempt to sell it for £320,000 in Christies' 1984 auction at Duxford was unsuccessful and Roland Fraissinet still owns and flies this rare bird.

One third of a million pounds in anyone's money is a sizeable sum, and as pointed out earlier the cost of running a Spitfire is high. Therefore a very sound financial base is essential, and many Spitfires are backed by large concerns as is the case with Mk 14 *RM689*, owned and displayed by Rolls-Royce. Built in the summer of 1944 this superb example, expertly maintained as befits such a renowned owner, was delivered to the Air Fighting Development Unit, Wittering, in August 1944. Following cockpit view trials it retired to Lyneham in November. March 1945 saw it received by 350 (Belgian) Squadron with whom it operated for a month before requiring major repair. From July 1945 until early 1946 it was again in Belgian hands. It spent two months with No 443 Squadron, RCAF, before being placed in store at 29 MU High Ercall. In February 1949 it was sold and became *G-ALGT*. Flying it from Hucknall, Rolls-Royce used it for Griffon development and flight test observation purposes until in the 1960s it adopted a role as a display aircraft, still flying as *G-ALGT*. It was following use in *The Battle of Britain* film that it appeared as '*RM619*' coded '*AP:D*' to represent a Mk 14 of No 130 (Punjab) Squadron. The aircraft now flies correctly identified as *RM689* and generally operates from Castle Donington.

There is surely no denying that the best of the Spitfires are those still part of the Royal Air Force. Tenderly cared for, deeply appreciated and maintained

So that no ill feeling should arise the Spitfires filmed in The Battle of Britain *carried 'impossible' squadron letters. N3310 shown is also a Mk V hybrid possibly with a Balliol powerplant.*

Above *In 1973 PR 19 PS853 was repainted in PR blue, and was photographed thus on 26 May of that year.*

Left *Just good friends, PR 19 PM631 of the Battle of Britain Memorial Flight wearing the meaningless identity 'AD:C' keeps good company with Hurricane LF363.*

Left *We owe a lot to that familiar Shuttleworth figure, the late Allen Wheeler who was the owner of G-AISU (seen here at the amazing 1951 Daily Express Hendon Show). Later it became again AB910.*

with considerable resources, the Battle of Britain Memorial Flight houses its four Spitfires — soon probably to become five — in a metal hangar close to the road on the western side of RAF Coningsby, Lincolnshire.

From a production point of view the newest of their Spitfires are the Mk 19s. Of these the most active of late has been *PM631* which in 1983-84 flew in black and white 'D-Day' markings and the markings of No 610 fighter squadron although it remains a reconnaissance aircraft. Built too late for operational service, it played a useful role with the Meteorological Flight at Hooton Park, and later Woodvale, where it formed part of the strength of the THUM Flight until June 1957. Then, the Flight's three Spitfires moved to Biggin Hill where the Memorial Flight formed on 11 July 1957. *PM631* has served with that Flight since then, except for special detachments and servicing away from base.

The Memorial Flight's other Mk XIX looks more its old self because it has been painted to represent one of the almost forgotten photo-reconnaissance Spitfires which played such a great part in the war effort. *PS853*, it arrived at Benson in January 1945 and in March joined No 16 Squadron, which was part of No 34 Wing responsible for photographic support to the British 2nd Army. It later served with 268 Squadron which on 19 September 1945 was renumbered 16 Squadron at Celle, Germany. When in 1946 the decision was made to equip No 16 Squadron with Tempests, *PS853* came home for storage at High Ercall and later Brize Norton. From there it joined the Meteorological Flight at Hooton Park and, like its Coningsby companion, became part of Woodvale's THUM Flight. After the three Mk 19s there were transferred to Biggin Hill, *PS853* became part of the Memorial Flight although it was considered to be inferior to its companions for which reason it was grounded at West Raynham in April 1958, partially taken apart to provide useful spares, then parked at the station's gate as *7548M*. A 1961 survey showed that it obviously had plenty to offer and it was transported to 19 MU St Athan. To the surprise of many, it returned to West Raynham in flying condition during November 1962. In April 1964 it was passed to the Battle of Britain Memorial Flight at Coltishall, and acquired a 'PR' colour scheme in 1973.

By good fortune the Battle of Britain Memorial Flight has acquired two very special Spitfires! It took many years to convince the powers of the land to save outstanding aeroplanes. Try as one might, it was a hard struggle and achieved little success until the late 1950s. Much was destroyed that nowadays would bring enormous delight to many people, and even massive financial reward to our governments ever looking for the means to make a quick million! By pure chance and not by design historic Spitfire Vb *AB910* survives for our joy.

This was the machine involved in that astonishing misfortune which overtook a WAAF, Margaret Horton, who was assisting in an engine run-up when a trainee pilot taxied forward with her clinging to the aircraft's tailplane. Even worse, and not knowing what had happened, the pilot took-off with Margaret still desperately clinging to the tailplane as he made a circuit. What she must have endured defies imagination.

Perusing a pilot's log book in 1952 I happened to come across an entry referring to his having flown at 53 OTU a Spitfire *AB910* by which was added '*QG:A* — the

Above *Engine shortage has long meant that, unlike a wartime Mk Vb, AB910 has had to have a Merlin adapted for a four-bladed propeller.*

Above right *P7350 soon acquired the correct 'UO' coding, and sits here at Waterbeach alongside its famous friend, the Lancaster PA474.*

Right *Most honour of all must surely go to the BBMF's Spitfire II, P7350, which for almost two decades gathered dust at Colerne only to break out of bondage to the freedom of the skies — thanks to the film* The Battle of Britain. *At first the RAF marked it 'ZH:T' — but those 266 Squadron letters were only carried by Typhoons.*

one which a WAAF clung to last week'. An official report of the event was compiled but it did not thus identify the Spitfire. It is always worthwhile to search through any available log book to hand for many contain information not recorded elsewhere, as was the case in respect of *AB910*.

A Spitfire Vb, *AB910* was first used by No 222 Squadron, which it joined at North Weald in July 1941 only to require repair in early September. Eventually, by way of 37 MU Burtonwood, it re-entered front line service by joining No 130 Squadron at Perranporth. From there it helped in December to escort heavy bombers making daylight raids upon Brest. In mid-January 1942 Westland Aircraft attended to *AB910*, and it was mid-June 1942 before it re-entered the front line, this time with No 133 (Eagle) Squadron stationed at Biggin Hill. Just before that Squadron was absorbed by the US Army Air Corps *AB910* was switched to 242 Squadron at Digby. Left behind when the Squadron left for Algeria, the Spitfire entered storage, first at Kirkbride and then Lyneham. July 1943 saw it return to Digby to serve briefly with 416 Squadron RCAF, for in July it passed to 402 Squadron RCAF, also Digby-based. With that squadron it operated until April 1944 when Spitfire IXs ousted the Vs. *AB910* joined 53 OTU at Kirton-in-Lindsey and, coded *'QG:A'*, flew from the satellite at Hibaldstow. It was here that Margaret Horton unwillingly made her flight.

The OTU closed on 15 May 1945 and *AB910* was immediately switched to 527 Squadron which undertook radar calibration duties from *AB910*'s favourite field,

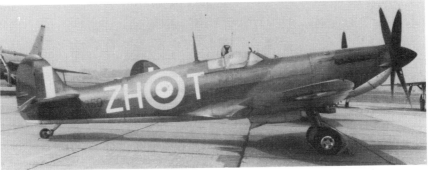

Digby. It moved with the Squadron to Watton, Norfolk, during November 1945 and when 527 Squadron disbanded there on 15 April 1946 *AB910* was passed to the Radio Warfare Establishment at Watton until No 29 MU High Ercall took control of the aircraft on 30 May 1946. Allen Wheeler, then a Group Captain, purchased *AB910* in July 1947 and the following October, as *G-AISU*, it was given a Certificate of Airworthiness at White Waltham. Allen Wheeler later sold it to Vickers who overhauled it and, marked '*QJ:J*', it was presented to the Battle of Britain Memorial Flight on 15 September 1965. Since then it has been involved in two flying accidents, one when landing at Duxford and a more serious occasion at Bex, Switzerland, when a Harvard collided with the parked Spitfire which needed major repairs as a result. In the course of those repairs much of a Mk IX, *MK732*, was absorbed by *AB910*. An interesting point is that the use of an ex-Balliol Merlin 32 has of late led to the aircraft flying with a four-bladed propeller, not a feature of the Mk V in its heyday.

The Battle of Britain Memorial Flight must surely be proudest of *P7350*, their oldest Spitfire and truly a Battle of Britain fighter. A Mk IIa, it was delivered to 6 MU, Brize Norton, in mid-August 1940 and to No 266 Squadron at Wittering possibly on 6 September. There it is thought to have become '*UO:T*'. October

Left *Tally Ho! — and which one is which as Spitfires, during the making of the film race across Debden?*

Right *In memory of 64 Squadron's brave battle days P7350 became 'SH:D'.*

Right *1985 saw P7350 paying tribute to the Royal Observer Corps (whose members so often enabled Spitfires to find the foe) in the markings 'EB:Z' of the 41 Squadron Spitfire presented to the RAF by the ROC.*

1940 saw it move into Hornchurch and 603 Squadron, hence its sometime '*XT*' coding. In late October 1940 it required extensive repair which put it out of use until mid-March 1941 when it joined No 616 Squadron at Tangmere. In April 1941 it was transferred to Hornchurch and No 64 Squadron, which operated it until early August, when it again had a major overhaul and repair. The Central Gunnery School, Sutton Bridge, received *P7350* in late April 1942 and from there it flew until further repair was needed in February 1943. From April 1943 to April 1944, *P7350* was on the strength of 57 OTU, based at its Boulmer satellite and coded '*VL*'. A flying accident on 22 April 1944 led to it entering storage at 39 MU Colerne in late July 1944.

There it languished until 1947 when it was sold for scrap to John Dale Ltd who, realizing its long history, returned it to RAF Colerne for preservation. There it was kept until 1967 and the inevitable participation in *The Battle of Britain* film.

Taken to Henlow, it was surveyed and clearly found to be ideal for flying sequences. In May 1968 it flew into Duxford registered as *G-AWIJ*, and was greeted with much delight for here was a real Battle of Britain Spitfire. It flew for many film sequences, and it was with considerable disbelief that some of those involved in the shooting heard that *P7350* was often to be seen at Duxford during September 1940! The 1968 summer weather turned so bad that the film's flying contingent forsook Duxford and in as exciting a formation as seen since the war, suddenly joined the Cambridge circuit. Customs cleared, they flew to the Perpignan area of France to complete the film there. Books were written following the astonishing filming, which dominated the British aviation scene in 1968. To see and hear Duxford echoing to so many Merlins was indeed to briefly embrace again a stupendous world long gone. I wonder if anything like it will, indeed can, happen again?

It's 1986, the superb Tornado F 2 is to hand — but the Spitfire is still the leader. Surely, no other aeroplane will ever remotely approach in fame and affection that great British triumph.

As for *P7350*, its future too was assured by its part in the film. After returning, to Bovingdon, the Spitfire joined the Coltishall-based Battle of Britain Memorial Flight in October 1968. The following April it was overhauled prior to display flying, and returned to Coltishall in fine form but erroneously marked as *'ZH:T.'* The letters *'ZH'* were not used by 266 Squadron until after it converted to Typhoons in 1942. Luckily a change to *'UO'* was possible, and later the aircraft wore *'QV:B'*, 19 Squadron's wartime lettering. Later it wore *'SH:D'* in memory of its 64 Squadron days. In 1985 its letters *'EB:Z'* recalled the Royal Observer Corps' 60th Anniversary, masquerading as a Spitfire which the Corps purchased for the RAF and 41 Squadron. Long may it delight us all!

★   ★   ★

'Now, running in from your left, ladies and gentlemen, you can see the formation of 19 Squadron Spitfires which are to demonstrate Air Drill to you.' It's Empire Air Day 1939, and through the rain they come, against a glowering grey backdrop. In trios, they pass, time-honoured style, before they turn in the west to come in echelon port. Impressive, fast, shapely but in their rough camouflage a disturbing sight as war seems fast approaching. In a year's time some will be locked in desperate conflict.

I sheltered beneath a visiting Whitley, to view 'the Spits' as best I could for my guess, proved true, was that this would be their last public display before the fight was on. Could it be that those lovely looking aeroplanes passing above were built to destroy and to kill?

Yet to kill what? ... All that seemed Hell-bent upon our destruction, or a fate too ghastly to even think of for long — the subjugation of our nation. Out of grim necessity had arisen this most beautiful form. Each, every one of us, has still a need to regard it with deep, deep gratitude, for the Spitfire is surely one of our most treasured creations.

Index